You've Been Chosen

You've Been Chosen

Thriving Through the Unexpected

CYNT MARSHALL

Ballantine Books

NEW YORK

Published in the United States by Ballantine Books, an imprint of Random House, a division of Penguin Random House LLC, New York.

BALLANTINE is a registered trademark and the colophon is a trademark of Penguin Random House LLC.

LIBRARY OF CONGRESS CATALOGING-IN-PUBLICATION DATA
Names: Marshall, Cynthia, author.
Title: You've been chosen: thriving through the unexpected /
by Cynt Marshall.
Description: First edition. | New York: Ballantine Books, [2022]
Identifiers: LCCN 2022000427 (print) | LCCN 2022000428 (ebook) |
ISBN 9780593359419 (hardcover; alk. paper) |
ISBN 9780593359426 (ebook)
Subjects: LCSH: Marshall, Cynthia, author. | African American
women executives—Biography. | African American businesspeople—
Biography. | Life change events.
Classification: LCC HC102.5.M26 A3 2022 (print) | LCC HC102.5.M26
(ebook) | DDC 338/.04092 [B]—dc23/eng/20220119
LC record available at https://lccn.loc.gov/2022000427
LC ebook record available at https://lccn.loc.gov/2022000428

Printed in the United States of America on acid-free paper

randomhousebooks.com

2 4 6 8 9 7 5 3 1

First Edition

Book design by Alexis Capitini

To my mother, Carolyn Gardner,
who showed me what it looks like to be chosen

Contents

You've Been Chosen

Your Voice of Power

It was the day before New Year's Eve. I had been puttering around our house all day, making sure everything was ready for my son Anthony's college friends, who would arrive later that afternoon for a traditional New Year's weekend of football games and black-eyed peas. I wanted to make sure these kids felt welcome, and was happy to see my Christmas decorations were still sparkling, filling every nook and cranny of our home with holiday cheer.

My four kids like to tease me, and my husband, Kenny, likes to complain, about my abundant—some might say *over*abundant—Christmas decorations. They think my holiday spirit is a little out of control, with stockings and trees and decorative pillows everywhere they look. And okay, I admit that forty-five bins of Christmas stuff can really fill up a house. We're not quite *Christmas with the Kranks,* but it's a lot. What can I say, I love Christmas, and I try to share that love.

The holiday music played through the house as I moved

around, competing for my attention along with the football game on TV and the member of my AT&T lobbying team on my work phone. As president of AT&T North Carolina, I'd already helped to set our major strategies to keep the company growing, but in these quiet days before the 2011 legislative session kicked in, I needed to review a few details.

On the surface, it looked like a normal day in the Christmas season for the Marshalls. But below the surface, there was an uneasy vibe in the air. Something troubled my spirit as I went from room to room to room, making sure towels were out, the beds were made, and the politicians were on board with my plans. As I listened to my colleague on the other end of my cellphone, part of me was on high alert for the sound of our house phone ringing. I was impatient to talk to a man I'd met only two weeks before but who had suddenly become one of the most important people in my life.

Finally, he called. There was some chitchat, and then Dr. Tyner said the words that still echo in my head today.

"I'm looking at your pathology report now, Cynthia, and I have news. It's bad and it's significant."

There were a lot of other words that followed, about a malignant tumor and lymph nodes and the urgency of scheduling more appointments. From some distant place, I heard him tell me that without chemotherapy I had, at best, a 25 percent chance of being here five years from now.

I was having trouble taking it all in. I'd been waiting all day— all week, really—for this call, but now I felt as if I were eavesdropping while Dr. Tyner talked to someone else, and I understood what people mean when they talk about out-of-body experiences. Clearly all of those bad words were describing someone else's body, not mine. Someone else's life. I had this intense urge to hang up the phone and go back to my work call and pretend this conversation never happened. All week I'd been pressing to talk to this man and hear his news. Now I wanted him to go away. I wanted to keep living the life I'd had when I was just handling my work. It was all I could do to hold on to the phone.

When Dr. Tyner finally said goodbye, I simply stood there. Kenny was beside me, his arms around me, but I felt as if this were someone else's body, someone else's life. Definitely someone else's tumor.

There was only one thing to do. With shaking hands, I called my mother.

I remember when she answered the phone that day, I had to strain to hear her traditional "Hey, honey," just above a whisper. "How you doing?" My mother is typically very soft-spoken.

I could barely hold it together as I told her about the pathology results and what Dr. Tyner told me. The word "cancer" might have been the hardest word I ever said. But my mother's voice didn't waver in her immediate response.

"This is for His glory!"

Her voice grew louder as she responded to my news. She shifted from my normal, soft-spoken mama to the woman who stood in front of her church on Sundays and preached the Word of the Lord as the Spirit worked in her. I could imagine her right hand, balled into a fist and bumping up and down, the way it did when she was at the pulpit.

This, I knew, was her voice of power.

You see, my mother is a saint, an angel, and a prayer warrior, all rolled into one. She loves Jesus like no one else I've ever met, so I shouldn't have been surprised that this was where she went in the face of unwelcome news. But I hadn't known about this cancer for very long, and I wasn't ready to face something that might kill me, even if it was for God's glory. Right then, I wanted a pity party.

I thought about hanging up the phone and calling someone who would be horrified and grief-stricken with me for a little while. But this was my mother, and I was raised to always honor my parents, and especially to listen to my mother when she got this tone. I held on to the phone and kept listening.

My mother told me she felt a message from the Lord drop into her spirit as soon as I said the word "cancer." She said that because I had a high-profile job, and because so many people knew me, my cancer journey would live itself out in the public eye, and people would benefit from watching my faith in action as I faced and beat it. There was no hesitation in her voice as she prophesied my eventual recovery, despite the prognosis. Her words were coming straight from heaven.

The more she talked, the more I felt my body stop shaking. I stopped crying. My mother wasn't crying, after all, so maybe I didn't need to, either.

I should get ready for the Lord to work, she told me, and call her back when I knew more about my next steps. She would fly from her home in California to help us in North Carolina. Her voice cracked only once, at the very end of the call, when she reminded me that "all sickness is not unto death," which is something Jesus says in the Gospel of John. She finished by saying again, "This is for His glory!"

∽

Her words were still ringing in my ears a week later when I started to understand just how much my journey through cancer would unfold in the public eye.

I wasn't a celebrity by any stretch, but by the time Dr. Tyner called, I'd been with AT&T for almost thirty years. I'd had eleven or twelve different jobs, each overseeing dozens, hundreds, or thousands of people. I'd been intentional about mentoring and building relationships, so I had a lot of friends within the company. Then, for the past three years, my new job as president of AT&T's state program had made me much more visible beyond our corporate office walls. Being the face and the voice of the company in North Carolina meant a lot of public appearances, community engagement, and interactions with local and regional media.

At first, as my news trickled out, the calls came from friends and colleagues all over the country, offering their support and wanting to help. Then the North Carolina media picked up on the story, and the next thing I knew, my cancer was on the front page of the Raleigh newspaper and getting talked about on the evening news. Calls started coming from people I didn't know.

That's the moment when I knew for sure that my mother's voice of power was right, as it always was. There was a reason that the Lord chose me to have this cancer, just as there was a reason for everything that happened in my life before it arrived. This was about to become a story much bigger than me.

❧

In the years since I found out I had cancer, plenty of people have asked me why I think I got sick in the first place. Why did this happen to me? Why does cancer happen to anyone?

I actually love that question, because it gives me a chance to share the story, once again, of my mother's prophetic words. My simple answer is that this happened to me because I was chosen.

If you knew anything about me before you picked up this book, it's probably that I've been blessed with many opportunities to serve others by being a "first." First Black senior class president of Kennedy High School in Richmond, California. One of the first Black cheerleaders at UC Berkeley. First Black sorority sister in our Delta Gamma chapter. First Black woman chair of the North Carolina Chamber of Commerce. First Black woman in a whole lot of boardrooms and leadership teams across the country. And today, first Black woman CEO of an NBA team. (Go, Mavs!)

But I'm *not* the first person to get cancer. Colon cancer like mine is the third most common cancer, and the American Cancer Society estimates that there are 150,000 new diagnosed cases of colorectal cancer every year. It's also the second most fatal cancer in the United States, and it disproportionately affects our Black brothers and sisters. Every week, it seems as if there is another heartbreaking headline about a tragic loss. (Rest in peace, Chadwick Boseman.)

I'm also *not* the first girl to grow up poor in the projects. *Not* the first daughter whose father threw punches. *Not* the first Black employee to be told she should change her looks, her voice, and herself if she wanted to advance. *Not* the first mother to grieve the death of her child.

My whole life story, when I look back at it, has shown me that there are rarely clear answers about why things happen in life. Sometimes that proverbial light at the end of the tunnel is actually the headlight of an oncoming train headed right for you. I've experienced abuse, death, racism, and cancer, and so I understand bad things happen to good people, and getting mad, or sad, or discouraged by that doesn't change anything.

By the time I found out about the nasty tumor in my colon, I had already been chosen for a lifetime full of stories about the ways the Lord provides. I'd been given blessings and opportunities beyond measure, but also my share of adversity. And yes, there were a few days when I asked Him, did I really need one more? Did I need to put my family, my friends, and my co-workers through all of this? But the answer He gave me was always yes. Cancer was going to be the story that would serve the most people, and serving others is what I believe I was put here to do.

So I said okay, first to God and then to my mother. I dug down past that out-of-body feeling to find my own voice of power, and I started to use it. I committed to being open about whatever happened next—the good, the great, the bad, and the ugly. The emails and blog posts you'll find in the pages that follow are the exact words that I wrote in the heat of the battle—complete with grammatical errors, inside references, and otherwise less-than-perfect communication.

I can't tell you the story of finding the "CAN" in cancer without also telling you all about the other things the Lord chose to bring to me, and the parts of my story that prepared and equipped me for the fight of my life—which in this case was actually fighting *for* my life. I can look now and see how the adversity and the blessings built on one another. That's what I hope you see throughout this book—what it has looked like for me to live and thrive through everything, what it has meant to keep my head up no matter what, and, most of all, how each event prepared me for what came next.

Bad things like cancer happen, but there's always a plan. I may never understand it, because I can't see the whole picture of how an individual's past, present, and future work together, but that doesn't mean the plan doesn't exist. Painful things are often what lead us into places we'd never go otherwise.

So the question I needed to ask when I got cancer wasn't why. That wouldn't get me anywhere. That's not my business.

The questions I needed to ask were: What will I do with what I have been given? How will I respond with grace? How will I respond with generosity? Where will this new path take me if I keep moving along it? And what can I take from this experience and offer back to the world as something good?

I hope that this book helps you see how all of *your* parts, even the hard parts, work together for good. I hope that wherever you are in life, you are encouraged to keep fighting the battle you're fighting right now. I hope that our time together reminds you to find your own voice of power and to step up and advocate for yourself. And mostly, if you've lost hope, I'm here to show you that you can make it through a lot more than you might expect.

You, too, have stories and experiences to tap into that will help you. You, too, have been equipped for whatever you're facing. You, too, have a choice in how you will respond. You, too, have been chosen.

1

Pay Attention

In the spring of 2010, not too long after my fiftieth birthday, I sat in a Dallas conference room with my colleagues, AT&T leaders from across the country, filling out the human performance expert Jack Groppel's Corporate Athlete assessment questionnaire. As the president of AT&T North Carolina, I was required to be there, but I didn't expect much to come from the session. I was sure I wouldn't find out anything new about myself. I knew me! I was in excellent emotional, mental, and spiritual health. I read and kept my mind sharp. I spent time with my family and friends to get the emotional support I needed. I was intentional about making time for prayer, going to church, and feeding my soul. As I remember it, my results were off the charts in those categories.

My physical health, though? I thought it would be my lowest score but figured it would still be decent. I used to be an athlete, and now as an executive and a mom, I was constantly on the go.

I'd already cut back on Ding Dongs and fried chicken. What else could they want from me?

I was partially right. Physical health was my lowest scoring area on Jack's assessment, but the score was far from decent. It was clear where I needed to put my attention.

A few months before, my primary care physician had given me a referral slip for a colonoscopy test, which he called a routine precaution for all his patients when they turned fifty. I'd thanked him and put the slip on my nightstand, figuring I'd get to it sooner or later. After all, I'd be fifty for a whole year. I had plenty of time.

I thought about that slip at the end of Jack's program, when we were told to all choose accountability buddies from within the group and then share with them one specific action step that we would take for improvement. I turned to Frank, a straight-talking executive from New Jersey, and told him I would get a colonoscopy. I was a busy woman, I reasoned, so I picked something I thought wouldn't require extra energy.

Over the following weeks and then months, Frank somehow always managed to call me when I was in the Starbucks drive-through. "Did you get that thing done yet?" he'd ask in his gravelly New York accent. I'd tell him no and change the subject.

Seven months and many Frank phone calls later, I finally got to say yes, the appointment was made, and so could we please talk about something else now? I scheduled my colonoscopy for December 14, the day before my fifty-first birthday. I was cutting that "get it done at fifty" close, but in my defense I schedule all of my routine medical checkups for my birthday week every year. I have an annual health plan that I stick to, and now it contained a colonoscopy "maintenance" box to check.

I still remember the anesthesia-induced "sleep" I had that day as the best I've ever had. I didn't feel a thing. When I woke up, though, the first thing I saw was Kenny standing over me. That wasn't normal. Kenny's not one to hover too close. Through my anesthesia haze I saw that he was frowning, biting his lip the way he does when he's bothered. I knew right away something wasn't right.

"Wife, we've got a problem," he told me, and then he stopped, not sure how to continue. "The doctor saw something he didn't like."

I didn't know how to respond to that, and my brain still wasn't working at its normal speed. I reached out toward the paper I could see in his hand. "What's that?"

After a second of hesitation—"Maybe you should read this later when you feel better"—Kenny relented and handed over the report from the gastroenterologist, who'd been called off to see another patient while I was still in recovery. He'd given Kenny copies of the scans they took, promising to call the next day to talk me through them.

I'm no doctor, but when I looked at the pictures of my body, even I could see the nasty-looking mass. It was not the birthday gift I was hoping for.

※

To be honest, the colonoscopy wasn't actually my first sign that something was wrong.

I'd been prone to sinus infections ever since I moved to North Carolina four years before, so I was used to swollen lymph nodes. When I felt something swelling in my neck a few months before, I didn't pay much attention. I just called my doctor for another round of super-duper antibiotics.

When I started inexplicably losing weight, I welcomed it and didn't ask questions. I complained sometimes to Kenny that I was feeling off and not like myself, but neither of us thought it was anything more than I had too much work, too much travel, and too many sinus infections. When Venessa, my chief of staff, mentioned that I looked tired and pale, I rearranged my travel schedule a little but kept going.

Then, in November, my kids all insisted that we go Black Friday shopping. It wasn't my favorite holiday tradition, but I agreed. We teamed up with a couple of my friends and their kids, and the crew was all at the mall by 4:00 A.M. As we were getting ready to go, I noticed my back hurt a little, but I wrote it off as the result of being on my feet in the kitchen the whole previous day, making Thanksgiving dinner.

The pain got steadily worse and harder to ignore, until about an hour later, when my son Anthony found me in front of a Macy's register, collapsed all the way to the floor in excruciating pain, but still holding up my credit card to the salesperson who was ringing up a new coat for my youngest, Alicia.

My conscientious boy was next to me in an instant, simultaneously helping me up and yelling at his sister for not doing something. He threatened to put me in a wheelchair until I agreed to stop shopping and wait in the car until he could round up the rest of the group.

I went to an urgent care clinic that afternoon, but they couldn't find anything specific wrong with me and sent me home, suggesting it was an early stage of diverticulitis. When I was still having trouble standing the next day, Kenny insisted I go to a hospital emergency room. There, a CT scan showed a lesion on my liver, but I left again with no real diagnosis. In fact, the ER doctor specifically told me he didn't think I had cancer, even though lower left back pain like mine is a symptom of colorectal cancer (as are weight loss, fatigue, and blood in the stool, which I'd also noticed but had dismissed recently).

The pain subsided after a few hours, and I went home and went on with my weekend.

❧

The day after my colonoscopy, my actual fifty-first birthday, I went back to the office. I have a tradition that I always work on my birthday, and not just because I don't want to miss my cake and ice cream at the lunchtime "surprise" party. Growing up poor taught me not to take my career for granted, and whenever I count my blessings, two near the top of the list are a great job and the ability to take care of my family.

Instead of enjoying ice cream with my team, though, I found myself stuck in a conference room, being grilled by auditors making a surprise visit. I'd been the president of AT&T North Carolina for almost four years at that point, and we had become a model program that other AT&T programs across the country followed. But that birthday meeting with the outside interrogators was unusually intense, and the way they asked about some of our business practices sounded more like an inquisition than a normal audit.

As a Black woman in corporate America, I had learned long ago that I would sometimes be treated as if I were unqualified or untrustworthy. It was an unfortunate reality. I sat with no notes in front of me, grateful for my good memory as I honestly answered all their questions and gave them facts.

I had nothing to hide and kept my cool, but after about five hours and one missed birthday party, my aggravation was starting to show. When my assistant stuck her head into the room to tell me that my doctor was on the phone, I gratefully took the opportunity to step out.

It was a case of "out of the frying pan and into the fire," because the gastroenterologist didn't have good birthday news for me, either. That out-of-body feeling struck as I stood in my office on my fifty-first birthday and heard for the first time that the nasty thing in the scan was a tumor in my colon and that I needed to talk to a surgeon right away. I don't think the doctor could use the word "cancer" without an official pathology report, but he was insistent that I get this "thing" looked at immediately. At the end of the call, he said again that it didn't look good.

I thanked him and hung up. After a quick call to Kenny to let him know what had happened, I went back to the inquisition much calmer than I'd been before. The auditors' questions were still ridiculous, but suddenly insignificant compared with what else I was facing.

To their credit, when I explained to the auditors that the call had come from a doctor, they offered to break for the day so I could make my appointments. I declined; postponing meant they would come back, and I needed to wrap this up so I could focus on what came next. I stayed in the meeting until they ran out of questions, sent them on their way, and then turned to my next task—making an appointment with Dr. Tyner, the surgeon my gastroenterologist recommended.

"Happy birthday to me," I told Kenny dryly that night when I finally got home. I didn't know what to think of all this hitting now. Was it a birthday gift or a birthday nightmare? Would I look back on my fifty-first birthday in the years to come and see the start of something tragic, or the start of something great? The jury was still out.

What I did feel right away, though, was that fifty-one was going to be very different than fifty had been.

❦

By the time Kenny and I sat down with Dr. Tyner that Friday afternoon, I'd spent three days looking at pictures of the tumor inside me. It looked nastier and more annoying every time I saw it. I was sure it was growing centimeters every hour. It needed to go, and it needed to go *soon.*

Dr. Tyner was pleasant and respectful, and appeared competent. I liked that he'd been practicing for more than twenty years and had experience with this type of tumor. I could see Kenny liked him, too. But things started to go sideways when he asked about our holiday plans. I explained we had originally thought we would go home to see our families in California, but obviously the trip was canceled.

The doctor looked perplexed. In his professional opinion, he said, my tumor was probably not cancerous, and there was no reason to interrupt our holidays. My surgery could wait until January or even February.

Oh, no. That didn't work for me. My own voice of power started to make itself heard.

I'm not a soft-spoken person like my mother, so when I take on "the voice," my volume doesn't change. But I lean in. I make eye contact. I let the person who's listening know what I know and how we're going to proceed.

I hadn't been born with a voice of power. It had taken a long time, and a lot of trial and error, to know how to trust my instincts and use my own voice to speak with both respect and advocacy, regardless of a person's title or outward presentation. I'd hesitated often when I was younger. Should I speak up? Should I sit back?

On that Friday afternoon, fifty-one years into my journey, I didn't hesitate. I leaned in and told Dr. Tyner that thirty years of leading teams all up and down the corporate ladder had taught me the only way to get things done is to act, and to act fast. I explained that I'd learned way back in Sunday school that my body was a temple and it was my job to take care of that temple. I had a nasty tumor inside me, and I wasn't willing to just leave it there, dirtying up the temple. I was willing to wait over the weekend, but this *thing* was going to come out of me no later than Monday.

Dr. Tyner was very polite. He agreed that the tumor was nasty, but told us he'd seen nastier. He repeated that this wasn't something for me to worry about. And besides, his schedule was fully booked for the next two weeks, and so were all of the hospital operating rooms in the city. Lots of people have elective surgeries right before the end of the year, I learned, and my tumor was going to have to compete for space with facelifts and tummy tucks.

None of that mattered. I was polite, too, but I explained that I wasn't leaving until we found a hospital that could handle this nasty tumor on Monday morning. We sat, smiling at each other and in a stalemate as the clock ticked. At one point, Dr. Tyner gave us a tour of his facility. I complimented his great medical library. Then I went back and sat in his office again. I had plans for that night—a birthday celebration with family and close friends—but I explained to the men in the room that plans can change.

Dr. Tyner studied me for a minute and then asked Kenny how long I was going to sit there.

"Get ready for a long night," my husband said. "She's not leaving until a surgery is scheduled for Monday." The doctor jokingly told Kenny he had a pretty good idea what my husband lives with daily. Kenny was too nice to explain that this was nothing.

I smiled at them both, prayed, and waited for good news. The doctor, reluctantly, told his staff to try to find an available operating room. They made several calls, to no avail. I kept sitting and silently praying.

An hour and a half later, a staff member came in to report that an operating room had opened up, and my surgery was scheduled for Monday, 6:00 A.M. It was even at WakeMed Cary Hospital, the hospital closest to our home.

My prayer became a prayer of thanksgiving.

2

It's Not Where You Live, but How You Live

Whenever I have a new boss, or colleague, or friend, I make it a point to explain to them up front who I am and how I was raised, because you can't understand the way I talk, or the way I act, without a few key pieces of my history.

First, my spiritual life is a vital part of who I am and how I communicate. My mother, as you've probably guessed, taught me from a young age just how important, and how powerful, prayer can be, and it's a lesson I've carried with me ever since.

Carolyn Estelle grew up as one of ten kids in Birmingham, Alabama, in a tiny two-bedroom house. Her father worked for the railroad and, according to the stories I was told, gave my grandmother just enough of his paycheck to feed the family before he drank the rest of it away.

My mother married my father, William Smith, when she was nineteen years old. He moved into her parents' house, and that's where they lived through the births of their first four children, including me.

Birmingham, in those days of Jim Crow, was a dangerous place for a Black family to live. In 1960, just months after I was born, my parents joined the Great Migration north, packing up their kids and getting on a train headed for Northern California, where my father had family. We settled near my father's sister in Richmond, in an area of the city called Easter Hill.

Growing up, I thought Easter Hill was great. I certainly never thought of it as "the projects." Those were tall, crowded apartment buildings, like where J.J. lived on the show *Good Times*. By the time I was old enough to remember, my family had moved into one of the "deluxe" units in the community—a single-story, four-bedroom townhouse with our own front door and backyard. Our unit was attached to other houses, and everyone parked their cars in a single big parking lot, rather than having their own driveways and garages, but compared with my mother's stories about her two-bedroom house with ten kids and two parents, we lived in luxury. I shared a bedroom with my younger sister, had my own space at the big kitchen table, and even enjoyed a study space in my open clothes closet.

And if sometimes my mother filled the dinner plates for her six children and then sat back, saying she wasn't hungry? I never paid much attention, and only realized years later that those were the nights when there wasn't enough food for her to eat, too.

Sure, there were more police in our neighborhood than where most of my school friends lived, and there were always young men hanging around on street corners who never seemed to go to school or have jobs. And one time, someone stole the Christmas lights my mother put on the bushes by our front door. (She loves holiday decorations, too; maybe that's where I get it from.) But like most kids, I didn't think too hard about where I lived. Easter Hill was home. There was a little grocery store down the hill where we could get our food, and a park where all of the kids could play football and tetherball. And on the days when my mother told us we couldn't be outside because of some conflict in the neighborhood, I had a houseful of siblings to play with.

My mother had a total of six kids in seven years—I was number four, the oldest of the "three little kids"—and we were all close. We'd set up our little record player in my bedroom and make up wild dance routines. I would be Gladys Knight, and my two brothers and youngest sister were the Pips. My older siblings would sometimes allow me to join their musical acts, and we'd have a party in our little house that rivaled anything we saw on TV. We danced and sang our way through the good times and the bad times. I still do.

∞

Carolyn Smith had plans for her four girls and two boys. Her love and her faith in us were unshakable, and because of her we never felt poor. "It's not where you live, but how you live," she would tell us. And more than that, "It's who you live for."

As soon as we arrived in the Bay Area, my mother got us settled in the Apostolic church where my uncle was a bishop, and despite everything we went through, I don't remember ever missing a Sunday service when I was growing up. Every week we'd put on our best clothes, line up, and walk together to the church, where the services would go for hours. My mother sang in the choir, and my brothers and sisters and I all sat up in the front row, where she could keep an eye on us. We'd better not even think about misbehaving, or sneaking out before the preacher started talking, either. Just a look from her was enough to keep us in line.

But church was never a punishment. We had God, and we had one another. Our mother showed us that with those two things, we could handle anything that came along. Through her, I learned that church was consistently a safe and peaceful place for us, in ways that our home often was not.

❧

When I was in third grade, for some reason our teacher asked each of us to talk about our fathers and what kinds of jobs they had. I stood up, all smart and proud, and said, "My daddy is a *hustler*."

I didn't know what that meant, of course. It was just something my father said all the time at home, and he said it with pride. He loved to talk about how he always had a hustle or a game going on. I knew when he was hustling, he was happy. And when he was happy, our house was peaceful.

I went on to tell the class about the top drawer of the dresser in my daddy's bedroom, and how inside there was this grassy stuff, and a little white gun that we weren't ever allowed to touch. I told them about how sometimes people outside would walk up to the window, which was at the back of the house. They would give him money, and he would get things out of the dresser for them.

I thought I had told the best story of anyone in my class that day, and I couldn't wait to get home and tell my parents that night. Of course, as I recounted my triumph, my father didn't look as happy as I felt. In fact, he looked scary when he turned to my mother. "Carolyn, you need to do something with her *right now*."

You see, my mother is a saint, but my father was not.

My father's anger was a terrible thing. William Smith was mean, and he took it out on whoever was around, mostly my mother. She was a victim of terrible domestic abuse for more than twenty years. She tried to keep the violence behind closed doors, away from us kids, but we all knew. We heard the screaming, and the beating, and her pleading for mercy. We saw her bruises and her blood, but not even my brothers and sisters and I knew just how bad it was. We had no idea how many times he almost killed her. How many times she thought she was about to die. How many serious head injuries she suffered. Even today, forty-five years later, the hair doesn't grow on top of my mother's head because of how many times my father ripped out whole chunks during one of his rages.

My father would beat his children sometimes, too. I grew up in constant fear, knowing he could erupt at any minute, over any little thing. He mostly stayed in his room, at the back of the house, doing who knows what, and we all tried to stay as far away from him as we could get.

There's one night in particular my siblings and I still talk about. I was little, probably not more than six or seven. My mother gathered us into the living room and told us, "Your father wants to talk to you." Those were terrifying words. No one knew what would come next.

My brothers and sisters and I all lined up on the couch, and I could feel my sister next to me shaking in fear, and I knew that I was, too.

My dad loomed up in front of us and in his big voice told us, "Your mother says I have to be nicer to you. Says that y'all are scared of me. Are you scared of me?" He was standing over us, each word getting louder.

"No," we all whispered, because that was what he wanted to hear. We didn't make eye contact with him, or with one another.

He got closer. "I said, are you scared of me?"

We made our voices a little louder. "No, Daddy. No, no, no."

He faced my mother. "See, Carolyn?" He said some other things to her that were not kind and do not need to be repeated.

My mother rarely stood up for herself, but she would die for her children. "Look at them, William. You're screaming. They're terrified. They're literally shaking in fear."

He swung back to us, and I sat on my hands so that he wouldn't see them trembling until he finally walked away, grumbling.

I don't know what my mother told my poor third-grade teacher to smooth things over after that day I explained hustling to a group of eight-year-olds. By then she was an expert at covering up my father's issues. She knew how to brush aside a concerned neighbor who saw her black eye and how to shoo all of her children out of sight when her husband had that certain look.

After that day, if anyone asked, I said my father was a barber, because he had done that for a while.

∽

Carolyn Smith worked two and sometimes three jobs to keep food on the table. That wasn't all that unusual in Easter Hill. Most of the women in my church and in my neighborhood worked to help support their families, so it's not something I ever questioned when I became a working mom myself.

But my mama didn't just provide. She *poured* herself into us. She made sure all six of us kids gathered for dinner every night. She gave us structure—not just the normal "no drinking, no drugs" kinds of rules. We had curfews. We had goals. We had chores. She kept us in extracurricular activities in school and at church, and if we weren't doing that, she had us learning things at home. Her love and her faith in us were unshakable, but she was no pushover, and she single-handedly kept us all in line. To this day, I don't know how she did it all, let alone always carried such a positive spirit.

Despite everything she faced with my dad, I never heard my mother complain or say a bad word about him or anyone else. He cussed like a sailor, but she never stooped to that. Instead, she prayed day and night.

The Bible wasn't just something that we talked about only in church. It was something that was part of our daily routines. My mother's faith sustained her every day, and she taught us how to make the Word of God practical for us. When we were old enough to join the youth choir, she would sit down and talk to us about the songs we sang and what they meant. The first time I really understood heaven as a place where we go after death was because of a conversation she had with us about "Goin' Up Yonder," a song by the Hawkins Family.

She taught us the Scriptures, or as she said it, "how to rightly divide the Word of God." Every summer, she set goals for us—not just educational and physical, but also spiritual. We studied books of the Bible and memorized verses. We made the Bible the go-to place for any question, any situation. She quizzed us on what verses meant. To this day, I can still whip out a reference to "some things are lawful, but not always expedient" when my kids try to argue, "Well, there's no rule about that, so we should be able to do it." Just because something is allowed, I tell them, doesn't make it the right thing to do.

Above everything else, my mother taught us to pray. We talked to the Lord about everything, all the time. As we got older, we would join her in fasting for days at a time while we prayed about specific things. We would attend what they called "shut-ins" at the church, where we would spend a whole night, or sometimes a couple of days, in prayer.

My mother's deep and abiding faith didn't stick with all of her children all the time. We all know the Bible, but at different times a few of my brothers and sisters had their periods of rebellion. I've made my own poor choices. There are no guarantees that a godly mother will raise godly children. But I'm here to testify that Carolyn Smith's faith made a deep imprint on me. I chose my path and made my personal commitment to the Lord as a teenager, and I have never looked back.

3

Be Prepared

——Original Message——
From: MARSHALL, CYNTHIA
Sent: Monday, January 03, 2011 2:44 PM
Subject: Message from Cynt Marshall

Some of you have probably heard by now that I was diagnosed last week with colon cancer. This finding was a result of my first colonoscopy, the day before my 51st birthday, December 14th. I had major surgery on December 20th to remove the diseased part of the colon and ultimately the pathology report found cancer in three lymph nodes and determined that I have Stage 3 colon cancer. Procedures are already scheduled for this week to determine more about the whereabouts of the cancer, etc. Chemotherapy will be a part of the treatment plan.

I will definitely beat this as I am uniquely equipped for

this battle. I have faith, good common sense, a detail oriented skill set, aggressiveness, a great employer and health plan, wonderful family and friends, and that includes all of YOU. I live in one of the best places in the country re: medical care so I am indeed blessed. And above all, I believe in the power of prayer. I will have just one more awesome testimony when this is all over and my three teenagers and husband will have a lot more faith in God.

Please keep me and my family in your thoughts and prayers. I've told my work team that the best thing they can do for me is to "keep it moving" and execute on our 2011 agenda. They will call on David and some of you for help. I will be keeping David and Jim posted on my condition regularly. Thanks in advance for your love, prayers and support. This will indeed be a happy new year!

Cynt

By the time we met Dr. Tyner on that December afternoon and scheduled my surgery, our holidays were in full swing. We'd canceled our flights to the Bay Area, our house—which Anthony jokingly called Marshall Manor—was fully decorated, and all the kids were squeezed into last-minute rehearsals for the Christmas programs at church. However, just like the surgeon and the hospital, I made room for my right hemicolectomy surgery at 6:00 A.M. on Monday.

Once again, I enjoyed the deep sleep of anesthesia while Dr. Tyner removed the tumor, along with a portion of my colon. I'm told everything went smoothly, but the pain was still intense. I guess that's what happens when they cut clean through multiple layers of tissue and muscles and remove part of an organ. I needed a morphine drip for the first twelve hours, but I cut it back as soon as I could and focused on getting home and back to Christmas.

When Dr. Tyner cheerfully entered my room on his Wednesday morning rounds, he found me sitting on top of the bed, dressed in my Cal Berkeley T-shirt, sweats, and hat. I even had my shoes on. "You look like you're going somewhere," he said.

I explained that I needed to be discharged so that I could see Anthony play the piano at the church program that night. My boy was home from his freshman year of college, and this mama needed to see her baby onstage. It was bad enough I'd missed the opening night performance.

Dr. Tyner, by this point, should have known what to expect when I decided I needed to do something. He should have heard that strength and power in my voice. Instead, he still patiently explained that it was too soon after my surgery. He expected me to need hospitalization for at least another day or two. I was recovering, he said, and I needed to complete a series of drills with the nurses before he would sign discharge papers, to show I was physically ready to go home.

I looked over at the nurse, who had been standing quietly by the door during his speech. She grinned and told him that I'd been up early that morning and had painfully but successfully performed the exit routine tests, including walking all the way up and down the hall. As far as the hospital was concerned, she said, that meant I was cleared for takeoff.

Dr. Tyner relented. As he reviewed my discharge instructions with me a couple of hours later, I asked when he would have the pathology report. He told me again that I didn't need to worry about it; he didn't think my tumor was cancerous.

"That might be true," I said. "But I still need a date." I wasn't being mean. I liked Dr. Tyner. He'd been very kind. But I understood he had other obligations and priorities. Taking care of my body was my responsibility, not his, and I knew it would be easy for my report to slip through the holiday-week cracks unless I leaned in, made eye contact, and showed him I wasn't leaving without an agreement about next steps. I was taking care of my temple.

We eventually determined the pathology report was scheduled to come back on Christmas Day, so Dr. Tyner would call me when his office opened again on December 26. I knew he was booked with back-to-back surgeries, and before I shuffled off to church with my family, I let him know I appreciated that he would take time.

∞

It felt good to be back in church that night. Kenny likes to say that I would be in church seven days a week if I could, and he's probably right. Churches simply feed my soul. I love them when they're quiet, and I love them when they're loud and full of people dancing and rejoicing. I love sitting in an empty sanctuary and praying, and I love surrounding myself with others as we listen and learn together. I was sad when Anthony got his driver's license and could get himself to his church activities, because that meant I didn't have an excuse to be there extra hours every week while he was in band practice.

When we moved to North Carolina, one of the first things we did was to find a church where we all felt comfortable. We found it a few miles from our home. The people were friendly. There were programs for my kids. If I couldn't be with my mother and my siblings that year to celebrate Christmas, being here with my church family was a close second choice, especially since I was there to see my boy use his talents. All those years of piano lessons had brought out Anthony's natural gift for music, and he gave those talents right back to the Lord by playing in our church bands whenever he was home from his freshman year at the University of North Carolina School of the Arts.

My body didn't let me forget what had happened, of course. I had to sit in the last row of the sanctuary, near the door, rather than my usual place right up front. That fresh surgical wound in my stomach made it hard to walk comfortably or naturally, and I wasn't there to draw attention to myself with some bent-over shuffle.

Not everyone was happy to see me. Cathy, the mother of Anthony's girlfriend and a nurse at the hospital where I'd had surgery, gave me an earful.

"Your immune system is shot," she told me bluntly, and I'd come straight to a place full of strangers and their germs. She told Kenny to go get the car to take me home. And she told me to stay there. I thought she was overreacting when she started lecturing me about my need to wear surgical gloves and a mask for a few weeks, to avoid infections. Looking back, though, I think the Lord was telling her that I needed a strong immune system for the days and months ahead.

The truth was, I was in a lot of pain. The surgery had cut right through my muscles; as I sat there, I could feel the injuries deep in my body. This was no minor procedure or surface-level cut that needed to heal, and I knew that Cathy was right. I needed to take this more seriously. I went home as instructed and discovered that I couldn't even climb the stairs to my own bedroom. For the first four days after my surgery, I had to camp out in our downstairs guest room.

Not that I was very good at resting. My mind was still on the outrageous work inquisition that had started on my birthday. The auditors were still at it, even during Christmas week and with me out on medical leave. And if they were pushing, I wasn't going to just lie in bed and let it happen. I kept getting up to find more documents or answer more emails, justifying it by saying the doctor had recommended getting up and moving around to help the healing process. Kenny finally snapped when he found me crawling up the stairs toward my home office, leaving a trail of blood from my post-surgery abdomen behind me.

⸎

To settle him down, I agreed to put work aside and focus on my overdue Christmas projects instead. I still had three hundred Christmas cards left to personalize and send, and suddenly we needed to wrap and mail a bunch of gifts to California we'd planned to deliver in person.

My best friend's daughter, Patrice, came over to help me finish the cards. She was a gem, entertaining me with jokes and stories while I stretched painfully across the bed and tried to personalize all those cards. I remember she was unusually chatty that day, probably so that we could both keep our minds off the imminent pathology report.

One benefit of staying in North Carolina for Christmas was that my nephew Cameron, who had just recently moved to Charlotte for work, could come up and spend Christmas Day with us. Almost everyone in our family—both mine and Kenny's—lived in the Bay Area, a place where I spent my whole life until we moved to North Carolina, and if we'd gone to California as planned, it would have left my sister's son all alone for the holidays. Instead, he had a place to celebrate, and he added to our festivities and helped to distract us all from the feeling of pins and needles as we waited for "the call."

I was still moving slowly that week as the surgical wound continued to heal, and I certainly wasn't up to making a big Christmas dinner for everyone. Instead, I found my joy in my enforced rest, sitting in the most comfortable chair and watching my family swirl around me.

Then, late on Christmas night, someone called us all to the front windows, where we saw a rare storm covering Raleigh in snow. I hobbled outside with everyone else to experience our first white Christmas. We were California folk after all, and my kids had only used their sleds and tubes on our annual trips to the mountains. But here was snow on Christmas Day! My heart filled as I watched my almost-grown kids jumping around in the wintry darkness, and told them that this must be the reason why God interrupted our trip back home. He meant for us to be home today to experience this gift.

∞

December 26 came and went. I was able to move back upstairs to sleep in my own bed, but there was no call from Dr. Tyner.

December 27, still no call. I'm sure it doesn't surprise you that I started calling him.

December 28, I left another message for my surgeon, but Still. No. Call.

December 29 was my daughter Shirley's sixteenth birthday. I was still in a lot of pain and distracted by my unfortunate work project, not to mention laser focused on getting those pathology results. I was so distracted, in fact, that I don't remember now how we celebrated. We'd planned to have a big party for her in California, but that had been postponed. I called my gastroenterologist and my primary care physician to ask for their help in tracking down the missing-in-action Dr. Tyner.

December 30 started with me making sure those Christmas decorations were still intact and the Marshall Manor bedrooms were in order for our incoming guests. Each person had their own Christmas stocking hanging on the fireplace and their own warm throw blanket and special Christmas socks waiting. A row of hot chocolate mugs lined the counter. My mama heart wanted to pour some extra love into these kids, even in the middle of my own uncertainty.

By the afternoon, I turned my attention back to work. Because I was the head of AT&T for our state, a major part of my job was working on public policy initiatives that would help my employer. Recent elections in the general assembly had opened doors for legislative changes in the next session, and by late afternoon I was on my cellphone, brainstorming with our lobbyist.

When our house phone rang, I checked the caller ID and saw that it was Dr. Tyner, finally returning my call. I asked the lobbyist to hold on while I answered the other phone.

Here's the brief exchange to my best recollection.

Dr. Tyner: I'm sorry it took so long to return your call. How are you feeling?

Me: A bit sore. I hope you're not working too hard and are

finding some time to enjoy the holidays, but what took you so long to call?

Dr. Tyner: I've had a lot of back-to-back surgeries.

And that's when he said it. "I have news. It's bad and it's significant."

He explained that the tumor was malignant and that I had cancer not just in my colon but in my lymph nodes and blood vessels.

Kenny, who had been lying on the couch watching the game on TV, saw something in my expression, jumped up, and came over to hold me while I talked.

At some point, as I listened to Dr. Tyner on the landline phone, I dropped my cellphone onto the family room carpet, and I never thought to pick it back up. Days later, I discovered that the lobbyist heard enough to understand that I was on the phone with a doctor, and knew it must be bad. He hung up and called a coworker to pray with him for whatever I was facing.

I heard Dr. Tyner tell me that this was not what he expected and that I needed chemotherapy right away. He acknowledged the odds might even be worse. It was a good thing I didn't put the surgery off, he acknowledged, because I didn't have a day to spare.

"You must hate me at this point," he said. "I didn't even think it was cancer."

That got my attention. I pulled myself together and told the contrite surgeon that actually he'd just gone up a few notches in my book. I was okay with his expressing his early opinion, because then he went on and did his job thoroughly even though he didn't think I was in danger. He biopsied everything he should have and didn't cut any corners. He didn't let his initial interpretation of a few photos bias him. What if he had skipped steps, thinking he already knew the outcome? I loved Dr. Tyner in that moment, and still do for his professionalism and expert approach during a difficult time.

Even though I still couldn't really feel my body, we got down to business.

He asked if I had an oncologist.

"Of course not. I have a gynecologist, but who keeps an oncologist handy?"

He gave me the name of someone to call, and I made an appointment to see Dr. Tyner again on Monday to start what he called "the process."

My tears started as soon as I hung up and had to repeat the word "cancer" to my husband. Kenny hugged me as tight as he had ever hugged me in the thirty-five years I'd known him. We'd already been through a lot together, my husband and I, so much that I knew the look he gave me. *This is going to be a hard one.* It was way too soon for the *But we got this* stage.

I took a breath and reached out for my anchors of faith, and the words of Psalm 91 filled my mind. It begins:

> Whoever dwells in the shelter of the Most High
> will rest in the shadow of the Almighty.
> I will say of the Lord, "He is my refuge and my
>   fortress,
> my God, in whom I trust."
> Surely he will save you
> from the fowler's snare
> and from the deadly pestilence.

And it ends:

> "Because he loves me," says the Lord, "I will
>   rescue him;
> I will protect him, for he acknowledges my name.
> He will call on me, and I will answer him;
> I will be with him in trouble,
> I will deliver him and honor him.
> With long life I will satisfy him
> and show him my salvation."

"Refuge," "trust," "long life" . . . those words ran together in my head. What was I supposed to do now? Did I need to start telling people? Who really needed to hear this bad news two days before New Year's Day? "Happy New Year, it's Cynt. I have cancer in my lymph nodes and blood vessels. I need to start chemotherapy soon or I might die."

That's when I called my mother. And the rest, as we say, is history.

4

Get Your Education

One night when I was eleven, my mother was getting all six of us kids together for dinner in the kitchen when there was a commotion at our front door. I heard my father come out of his room and go to the living room. My mother, sensing trouble, hurried us all into the bedroom at the back of the house, which I shared with my younger sister, Ros. She pulled the door behind us, but it didn't close all the way. She didn't notice when I slipped back out and up the hall.

I wasn't trying to get into trouble that night. I was just at that age where I always wanted to know what was going on, and I'd heard enough raised voices in this house that it didn't occur to me to be scared or even cautious.

I crept out to the living room, staying behind my father so he couldn't see me. He stood by the front door, arguing with a young man I'll call Michael, whom I recognized from the neighborhood. Michael's mother went to church with us, but everyone knew her son was always getting into trouble and running with what she called "the wrong crowd." Most of what I knew about him came from hearing her prayers.

I never found out why Michael came to the door that night. I don't know if he and my dad were doing some hustle or deal together, or if he was looking to start random trouble and rode up on the wrong person that day. But by the time I got to the room, he clearly meant business.

I saw the silver pistol in his hand at the same moment Michael saw me standing there, watching him. My heart stopped. Without saying anything, he shifted his body slightly. It didn't register to my eleven-year-old mind, but years later, replaying the scene over and over, I realized that he moved so that he could aim his silver gun right at me.

It wasn't the first time I'd seen a gun, but it was the first time I'd faced one.

My dad must have noticed Michael move and looked back to find me standing behind him. He also saw what I didn't—that the gun was pointed down toward me. Without saying a single word, my father pulled his own gun out and shot Michael in the head.

It all happened that fast.

After the pop of my father's gun there was a lot of screaming, and my mother appeared and pulled me back to the bedroom. There was no time to dwell on what I'd just seen, because I was suddenly surrounded by my siblings. Everything sped up. My father rushed back to his room, probably to dispose of whatever he needed to before the police showed up. My mother ran to the kitchen to call an ambulance. Michael lay near our doorstep, bleeding from the head until it arrived. It was chaos.

My father acted that night in self-defense, and also in my defense. My dad had been in the army before he married my mother. He used to brag about being trained as a sharpshooter, and his shot that night was almost point-blank. I believe he could have easily killed the angry young man on our front step, but he didn't.

Michael lost an eye, but much to his mother's relief he survived the night.

Shootings were rare back then, even in the projects, but not so unusual that our incident in Easter Hill made the news or drew any outside attention. It was just another example of violence in the projects. Still, the police, acting out of an abundance of caution, told my mother that she should lock down the rest of us while they took my father to the station overnight and wrote up their report. Michael had shown up at our house alone, and seemed to be acting on his own, but we all knew he had brothers and friends, and they worried about somebody coming after one of William's kids as retribution.

That seemed silly to me. I wasn't afraid of Michael or his family. We knew them. We went to church with these people. I couldn't imagine any of them trying to hurt me. It was only years later, at about the same time I realized Michael deliberately pointed that gun at me, that I started to consider how much violence I'd seen in my home by that point and how accustomed I was to living in constant fear of my father. Maybe that's why I didn't feel more upset.

When everything quieted down that night, however, I noticed I was physically shaking, and that continued for days. My mother and father hugged me and consoled me. They were worried about all of us, emotionally and physically. My body was in shock, even if my mind didn't have the words to explain it. And so I fixated on not being able to go to school. That, when I was eleven, seemed worse than seeing that gun pointed at my head.

∞

School was important to my mother and father, and so it was important to their children. All six of us went to school, no matter what, just as we went to church. Structure and routine were our ways of handling my father's unpredictable outbursts. Education and faith were our paths out of the projects.

I thrived on my mother's insistence on routine. I loved being active and busy, and I really loved school. I loved my teachers, and the textbooks, and all of the things I got to learn every day. I loved taking math tests. If church was always important to me, by then school was my *world*.

I always tell people that my mother put two books in my hands when I was very young—a math book and a Bible. These, she told me, were my tickets to a better life. She'd tried to get more education herself, enrolling in business college after high school, but starting a family and then the family's move to California cut that short. I think the disappointment of not finishing that degree is part of why she was so determined her kids would go to college someday. She saw this as our way out, a chance for something more than what she had.

On report card days, my mother would meet each of us kids at the door after school. It didn't matter how many jobs she was working at the time; we knew we'd come home to find her standing right at the front door with a basket. We'd put our report cards into the basket as soon as we walked in the door, and then when everyone was together, we'd gather around the big table. She'd open each report card and praise the recipient. She made getting grades into a big deal, a celebration of another quarter of learning and achievement.

She understood her children and knew what we were capable of. If it was just barely getting a passing grade, then she would praise the C. For me, we both knew my best was straight A's. School came naturally to me. Numbers, especially, just always made sense. One of my favorite things to do was to sit in the backseat of my parents' car and add up the numbers on the license plates of other cars passing by.

I have so much gratitude for the public school teachers of Richmond, California, who stepped into the lives of kids like me—kids with a lot of potential, but also with a lot of distractions at home—and provided us with safe places and extra encouragement. In elementary school, there was a teacher who let us all come to his classroom—I still remember it was room 17—after school for a little informal dance party to let off stress and take our minds off anything that was happening outside the walls. Dancing was how we stayed out of trouble, and to this day I love to dance.

School was where I was safe and welcome, but it's also where I could achieve.

∽

The day after the shooting, my mother took the advice of the police and kept us out of school. She gathered us all around the kitchen table and had us get out our books, and we did "school" right there at home. My siblings seemed to do just fine with this temporary homeschooling condition.

But it wasn't the same for me. I missed my teachers and my friends. Plus, family and neighbors were knocking on our door all day, wanting to know what happened. Some wanted to pray, and some wanted to gossip. Even Michael's mother came over to talk with my mother, to make sure things were all right between our families.

I couldn't be cooped up in the middle of the drama. Being home was like a punishment.

I wailed and cried all through that first "lockdown" day, driving myself to the edge of an anxiety attack and probably making the rest of my family crazy. My mother could see it. Being locked down clearly wasn't going to work for me. I needed normalcy, not punishment. I hadn't done anything wrong.

My mother called a local cop on the Easter Hill beat, a man named Darryl Prater, and explained the situation and how upset I was. Could he find some way for me to go to school and still be safe?

He could and he did. In fact, while my siblings all stayed home and did their work at the kitchen table, Officer Prater personally escorted me to and from seventh grade every day for the rest of the school year.

Every morning he would come to our door, wearing his uniform, and ask how I wanted to go to school that day. Sometimes, I wanted to ride the bus, and so Officer Prater would ride the school bus with me. Other times, I told him I wanted to ride in his squad car, and so he'd open the front passenger door for me and drive me to school as if he were my personal chauffeur. My only disappointment was that he never agreed to turn on the lights and siren. At the end of the day, Officer Prater would bring me back home the same way.

He was so friendly and encouraging that I never felt it was weird to have a police escort to junior high. I never felt ashamed to have a father who shot a man. He defended his family. I just felt grateful to be allowed to move forward, to do what I was supposed to be doing, to not let my circumstances derail me. Bad things had happened, but they wouldn't keep me from handling my business.

Forty years later, that was still my attitude. There were some things I could control, and some things I couldn't. But whatever happened, I handled my business. I had to have a plan and I had to keep moving. Perhaps this is where I learned that sometimes the light at the end of the tunnel is a train and that bad things do happen to good people. Life is not necessarily about what happens to us but about how we respond.

5

Make a Plan

Wednesday, January 12, 2011

Happy New Year to all of my family and friends. I know this will be a great year and beating cancer will be one of my big testimonies this summer! Since receiving the diagnosis of stage 3 colon cancer on December 30th, I have undergone many scans, MRIs, doctor visits, etc. The scans and MRI results have been positive, and if all goes well over the next few days, I will begin six months of chemotherapy next week.

I am honored that the Lord has chosen me for this journey and excited that all of you are on this journey with me. We will have quite a story to tell. Just when you thought we had run out of speech material . . . here we go.

I have been feasting on the words from Psalm 91 regarding God's protection. I know I am in His hands. Thank you for all of your love, prayers, cards, phone calls, emails, food, gifts and visits. I am encouraged and ready for this battle. Enough about me today . . . don't forget Haiti my friends. One year later, the Lord is still showing himself faithful. Arizona needs our prayers too. I love YOU!

Cynt

On that New Year's Eve eve to remember, Kenny and I started to rally the troops. First I called our pastor and asked him to come over to pray with us. Then I called my posse—my four best friends in North Carolina. "Come over," I said. "We need you."

I wanted to tell the kids before everyone arrived. Kenny wanted to wait. It was a holiday. Anthony's friends were visiting. What was the rush? But I knew they were old enough to be perceptive. They obviously already knew that we were waiting for test results from my surgery, and they'd know something wasn't right as soon as the pastor came knocking on the door on December 30. A pastor coming on Christmas Eve? Maybe. But what pastor makes house calls for New Year's? Something was up, and I didn't want them hearing the news from anyone else. We had to get ahead of it. We had to keep moving.

Kenny just shook his head. "They're not going to take it well," he said. "This family cannot function without you, and these kids are going to have the same first reaction I did: 'What happens if Mom isn't here?'"

I told him that he was being ridiculous. No one's mind needed to go there. I wasn't going anywhere. I wasn't going to die. I gave him a whole speech about how our kids were going to kick in and learn from this. I told him to trust them, and that they'd be better for the experience.

Kenny wasn't buying it. "Shirley's going to wig out," he said. "She's not going to want to hear your mapped-out plan."

We gathered our three kids around the kitchen table, and I

seated them strategically, based on what I thought they would need emotionally, with Alicia, the youngest, in the middle. We called Rickey, our oldest who was already grown and living in Houston, and put him on speakerphone. Then, just as I planned, I calmly told them that the pastor was on his way over to pray with us because we'd just found out I had cancer. "I know I'm going to be fine," I said for the first of many times, but I was also honest that Dad and I had no clue what to expect would happen next. None of us had experienced cancer before. I shared the encouragement their grandmother had just given me, and I asked them to be my prayer warriors. We are the Marshalls, after all, praying people who know how to face adversity.

"Don't start wigging out on me now," I told them.

Just as Kenny predicted, Shirley wasn't having it. At sixteen, she was at the stage that was all drama, all the time. Wigging out is what that girl did best. "You're going to die!" she wailed. Nothing I said could change her mind. She'd watched the movie *Stepmom* on TV, the one where Julia Roberts has an awkward relationship with her husband's kids until their mom gets cancer, and I guess that made her an expert on the disease. The girl was a mess.

I made the mistake of glancing at Kenny, and he was smirking. He knew he'd called it correctly. For a second, I had a hard time getting my words out.

"What, and now you two think this is funny?" Shirley snapped at us. Poor girl. She didn't know about the hours her parents had already spent together, talking through what was happening. She hadn't seen Kenny's tears or heard his pessimistic perspective, so much like her own. And my plan was certainly not helping her calm down.

Anthony, on the other hand, is an optimist like me. His glass isn't just half-full; it's always running over. He agreed right away that we'd all be fine. Pointing around at the Christmas decorations all over the house, he told Shirley, "Dad always says we should enjoy these decorations, because if anything ever happens to Mom, 'we ain't doing all of this!'" At eighteen, he did a pretty good impression of his father. "God's not going to take Mom away from us and leave us with just Dad, because He knows we need Christmas."

That gave us all—even my husband the Grinch, who does grumble and complain his way through decorating my winter wonderland every year—a much-needed laugh.

Rickey's long-distance voice stayed calm and practical as always. At twenty-seven, he had a lot of questions about next steps—when the chemo would start, whether he should come to North Carolina, that kind of thing. His way of handling a surprise had always been to gather information and make a plan.

And Alicia? That poor girl didn't know what to think. Our almost thirteen-year-old's eyes were wide and serious as she watched her brother and sister bicker, looking back and forth as if she didn't know whom to believe. Would this really be okay? At one point she reached out and grabbed Shirley's hand to comfort her, but in the whole conversation she never said a word.

We talked. We hugged. We prayed.

When we were done, my positive, upbeat, newly adult son headed back to his space in the basement, where his college friends were waiting. Kenny and I had met them a few times already, when we visited Anthony on campus, and I knew they were good kids. I'd even pulled them aside earlier and warned them that we were going to tell Anthony something that might upset him. I didn't say what it was, but I asked them to encourage him and embrace him when we were done. I trusted them to know how to handle it.

When he went downstairs, before the door even closed behind him, I heard him start to cry, and I saw his friends surrounding him with open arms. I thought about how Dr. Tyner's delayed phone call meant that we got the hard news on the day when Anthony had the support he needed.

∞

We all need people to help us through the tough times. That night Marshall Manor filled up quickly with friends we could trust, and they came again the next day, and then the next, as we settled into our new reality.

When the Marshalls moved from California, where our families and churches and safety net were, to the unknown state of North Carolina, one of my first priorities was finding the group of women who would have my back. I was always close to my three sisters, and then, when I went to Berkeley, I pledged Delta Gamma and found the support and camaraderie that I needed. Now I was far from the Bay Area and my support network; I knew I couldn't be alone.

And so the Lord brought me "the posse"—Hokey, Yvonne, Lisa, and Bev—four women who were also trying to take care of themselves and their families. By the time they came to my house the night I found out about the cancer, we'd already seen one another through divorces, job crises, dramas with the kids, and all of the ups and downs of life. We were comfortable and safe together, watching movies on Friday nights and opening presents on Christmas afternoon. We had a group text thread that blew up our phones several times every day. We sat on cold metal bleachers together watching our kids' soccer matches and swim meets, and we sat in church together, and we gathered around holiday dinner tables. Once a year, the posse would even leave kids and jobs and husbands behind and go to the Bahamas together.

So when I called on the day before New Year's Eve and said "I need you," they were all there in a heartbeat.

Hokey, who had once been a nurse in an oncology ward, showed up with grocery bags full of leafy green things and, without asking, started using my blender to make gross blueberry "anticancer" milkshakes. She kept pushing me to drink one because it was "rich in antioxidants and ingredients that help prevent cancer." I rolled my eyes and told her it was too late for that. I already had cancer.

Lisa and Bev were as stable as rocks that night. They arrived ready to pray and to search the internet for the information I didn't have yet, which was probably what I needed most. Lisa's husband, Rick, had had Hodgkin's lymphoma when he was in his twenties, and so she became the closest thing to an expert we had in those early hours. She knew what questions to ask to help draw out what Dr. Tyner had told me and what terms to search online to help us all understand what I was facing.

But it was my friend Yvonne who truly stole the show. Always prone to drama and speaking her mind, she threw herself onto my couch as soon as she arrived, totally zoned out and unable to function, and from then on she mostly just got in people's way. Finding out that I was this sick wiped her out, and also took away a lot of the energy from what was supposed to be my pity party. At one point Kenny pulled me aside to ask, "You're the one with cancer, right?"

We gave her a hard time, especially when she started bossing Kenny around, but we knew and loved Yvonne for who she was, and this kind of response wasn't a surprise to anyone. Everyone processes bad news in their own ways, and different people have different roles they want to play. We all offer what we can from that space. Yvonne's offering, it seemed, included telling Kenny to make her cocktails.

When her dramatics really started getting on everyone's nerves, I told her to stop acting as if this were a séance and sent her out for hamburgers. When she came back, I staged my rebellion. "No more healthy milkshakes," I told Hokey. "We might be clogging up our arteries, but at least if we die, we die happy." After all, I'd given up my fried chicken and Ding Dongs, and look where that got me. Chemo, according to Bev and Lisa's research, was going to rob me of my taste buds for a while, so for a night I was going to enjoy myself.

❧

Once I had time to process the news, I knew that my mother was right and I was going to beat cancer. While my friends were still lying about on my couches, and the rest of the world watched football and ate black-eyed peas on New Year's Day, I sat at the computer and got down to business. I wanted to know everything about the disease that had somehow found its way to our house. Literally, MY house. MY body. MY world.

The only way I could make sense of what was happening was to approach it the way I would approach any big project at work, so I took all of the focused, people-driven, optimistic energy I usually reserved for major work initiatives, and I aimed it at cancer. I gathered the information, laid it all out, and made a plan, and then—most important—I figured out how to get it moving. My routines were about to change, my structures would look different, but I could adapt. Hard work and prayer had gotten me this far, and I figured they would get me through this as well.

The first thing, I decided, was that I was going to focus on only the "CAN" in cancer. I was not going to dwell on the tumor—how I got it or whether I could have done something differently. That was in the past. I was going to focus on what would happen next.

I heard my mother's voice assuring me I was going to beat it. That the Lord would show up, just as He always had. I was going to live, and nothing was going to change that. I set my voice to my intention. "I CAN, I CAN, I CAN!" I told anyone who would listen. I would do this. I can beat this. I can handle whatever this brings.

Plenty of people since then have asked where that certainty came from. All I can say is that my history, and a lifetime of personal experiences, had prepared me. Time after time, I saw that when people like my mother were down, they could dig deep, hold fast to hope, focus on solutions, shout out for help, and *then get up*. Pulled up by other people or spiritual forces, they started to live again. And so it never occurred to me that I couldn't do the same. I might have been wounded and wobbly, but I knew that whenever I'd been knocked down, I always got up. Knocked down but never knocked out.

⚬

Having cancer was obviously going to affect my ability to do my job, so one of the first things I did was call my boss, David, on New Year's Eve so that we could get ahead of any rumors. He was immediately supportive. A few hours later (still on New Year's Eve) *his* boss, Jim, called me to offer his own concern and support. Then Jim's boss, the chairman and CEO of all of AT&T, Randall Stephenson, called. They all made it crystal clear that I would receive the best care possible and that the company would do whatever was necessary to support me and my family, starting with a referral to MD Anderson for treatment.

MD what? I'd never heard of Houston's famous hospital, and at one point I even told Kenny I didn't understand why AT&T wanted me to go somewhere in Maryland. A quick Google search straightened me out and introduced me to one of the top-ranked hospitals for cancer care in the country, but opened up a new problem. Houston? I told my bosses that while the offer was incredibly gracious, I couldn't leave my kids for months and go off to face cancer alone in Texas. And even though our company was headquartered in Texas and offered great support, I would do this right here at the top-tier facilities in the Tar Heel State. I called the oncologist Dr. Tyner recommended, and set up an appointment.

⚬

I knew that it wouldn't be possible to keep my health situation a secret for long, given my position. When you're the face of a major company, as I was, the media is always looking for insight into what's new and what's changing. An executive's personal life can affect the way they lead, which in turn affects everything from jobs to shareholder returns. My cancer, according to one line of thinking, was really a business story about how a major company was being led.

I knew the best I could hope for was a couple of weeks of privacy while I processed the situation, communicated with key constituents, and solidified my treatment plan. The trouble was that I was already scheduled to emcee a major chamber of commerce event—the annual economic forecast luncheon—on the Monday morning after I found out about the cancer. I also needed to meet with my doctors that day.

We'd been preparing every detail of this event for months. I'd recently been elected the first Black woman chair of the North Carolina Chamber of Commerce, which was a big deal not just to me but to the community. And this was a major event, with several hundred of the most influential business leaders in the state and lots of press coverage. I was supposed to not just emcee but also give an award to the former White House chief of staff Erskine Bowles. We all knew my absence was going to be noticed and required flawless handling to avoid a media frenzy.

After a flurry of phone calls and a handful of people sworn to secrecy, my friend the powerhouse real estate CEO Billie Redmond agreed to pinch-hit for me as emcee. She would run the show and present the award while deflecting any questions about my absence. It was an enormous favor to ask, but she didn't hesitate before she said yes.

If asked, Billie planned to explain that I had a family emergency and couldn't be at the luncheon, but I would be at future events. It was supposed to be that simple. Of course, it wasn't.

There was a buzz in the room when Billie announced my absence, but the program went forward without a flaw. By all accounts she was a fantastic emcee. After the event, though, an exhausted Billie found herself surrounded by local reporters who weren't buying the "family emergency" line. I worked regularly with the local press, and they knew me. They knew my family. Was there a death in the family, or did something happen over the holidays? Did she have to go to California? Is she okay? The piece of my plan that I hadn't considered was that people in the press would be personally concerned about me.

As the reporters kept doing their reporter thing, asking questions, Billie burst into tears. She finally broke, with the cameras still rolling. "Cancer," she told them, and it was out there.

One of the things I love about North Carolina is how genuinely kind everyone is, including the press. I'd experienced it myself many times over the past few years and had learned to really enjoy and appreciate my interactions with the journalists who dedicated themselves to seeking and sharing truth. We'd become friends, even. As soon as Billie said "cancer" that day, the swarm of media turned into a group of supportive friends. They were shocked. They hugged her. They turned off their cameras and swore one another to secrecy. This wasn't public news yet, and they respected that. They coordinated with my press office to help me make my situation public in the way that was best for everyone. It wasn't just in my mind. These people had really become my friends, my allies. In North Carolina, I had joined a community that cared about me and my family first, and my title and company second.

❧

At almost the same hour that Billie was talking to the press, Kenny and I were in Dr. Tyner's office again. The air in the room had changed since our first time there, when the surgeon had told us not to worry. Now he explained in detail that I had stage 3 invasive cancer, one lymph node away from stage 4, with what's called a vascular invasion, as well as a six-millimeter lesion on my liver. There were discussions about various treatment options, but in the end we all agreed that in my situation chemo was essential.

My new oncologist, Dr. Charlie Eisenbeis, talked to me about my options. Given how advanced the cancer was, he recommended a regimen of twelve chemo treatments, once every two weeks for six months. I would come in on Tuesday mornings for labs and a four-hour round of chemo, then carry a portable pump for forty-eight more hours of infusion. I'd go back to the cancer center on Thursdays to remove the pump and get more blood work. He described the drugs he would use and the side effects they would cause.

"What happens if I don't do it?" I asked him. After all, the surgery had removed the tumor. Part of me wanted that to be the end of it and for this to be over.

He looked at me long and hard. "Worst case? You could die." Stage 3 meant that the cancer had probably traveled to other parts of my body, he said. Without chemo, there was a significant chance I wouldn't be around much longer.

When he said that, all of my fuzziness disappeared. This was real. If I was going to survive—and I knew I would—we were doing this. I signed up for chemo and started to get ready.

6

Searching for Peace

If my mother taught me the power of prayer and the importance of education, William Smith taught me to overcome adversity.

My father lived with us until I was fifteen years old, and every year had its own series of explosions. It wasn't just the incident with Michael. He would regularly explode over just about any mistake or insult, real or imagined, leaving my mother bloody and my siblings and me—now all teenagers—both angry and terrified. But nothing captures life with my father quite like what happened in the summer of 1975.

I had just finished my sophomore year of high school, and my older brother, Phil, was getting ready to graduate from high school. None of us knew it, but that summer my mother was also secretly filing for a divorce.

She'd stayed with my father for twenty years of physical and emotional abuse, and she'd held it together because she desperately wanted her children to grow up with a father. Even when her doctor told her she was on the verge of a nervous breakdown, she stayed. But in 1975, my father started openly running around with another woman, and my mother just couldn't take it anymore. She was *done*.

She knew that if she told my father she was leaving him, he would explode, and there was no way my mother was going to provoke that scene before my brother's graduation. Getting a diploma was the best and biggest thing you could do in my mother's eyes, and she was determined to celebrate Phil with no distractions. We would have a joyous day.

Back then, though, if you wanted to get divorced, the law said you had to post a public notice in the newspaper. My mother's legal aid attorney promised her that the notice wouldn't come out before the graduation. But there was a mix-up at the paper, and on the day of the graduation there was her divorce announcement, printed for all the world to see.

We were all at home that afternoon, getting ready to go to the ceremony. My mother was in the kitchen, preparing food for the party we'd have at the house later. My brother was already wearing his gown, and I was in my room, getting dressed in my navy palazzo pants and a little red blazer over a frilly white blouse (*very* 1975), when my father came slamming into the house, yelling for my mother. That wasn't unusual, and she didn't know about the newspaper posting, so she went back to their room to see what he wanted.

As soon as she reached the door, all hell broke loose. The screaming and the thumping started almost before the door closed. We'd seen his rages before, but I could tell right away this was over-the-top crazy.

There were four of us kids in the house, and we all rushed down the hall and tried to get him away from her, but my father wasn't hearing any of it. When we got into the room, my mother's face was already covered in blood, and she was pleading with him to stop, to just wait until after the graduation. Instead, he turned and came at us, too, and I saw a rage in his eyes worse than anything I'd seen in him before. Someone, I still don't know who, finally called the police, because this wasn't something we could handle on our own.

It was a different time. Back then in Easter Hill, the police didn't usually arrest a man if he was beating his family. They just separated everyone until things calmed down. But that day, anyone could see my father was out of control, and things weren't going to calm down anytime soon. He was screaming, right in front of the police, that he was going to kill my mother, then kill all of us. They held him back. One officer told us to pack some things and go somewhere safe. I was shaking, crying, scared to death, and ready to run to the end of the earth to get away from this violent man, but my mother was still entirely focused on my brother. "We can't leave now," she kept telling them. "We have to go to the graduation."

That's how important education is to my mother.

That's how important it was not to let anything keep her from her goals.

Eventually, the police agreed to escort us to the graduation ceremony, as long as we promised to go somewhere safe after that. One patrol car left right away with my brother so he could meet his class and get in line. The rest of us grabbed whatever we could from our rooms while my mother washed the blood off her face and cleaned herself up. Then another police car took my mother, me, and my two younger siblings to the arena, leaving my father at home, still yelling and screaming about all the things he would do to us.

The officers stood in the back throughout the ceremony, visible but out of the way, just to make sure my father didn't show up. When the last graduate had their diploma and the last photo was taken, my brother went off with his friends to celebrate his big night, and the police escorted the rest of us—my mom and her three youngest kids, including me—to my oldest sister's apartment. Cassandra was just nineteen but already married—mostly as a way to get away from my father—and she and her new husband lived in a little one-bedroom place in a different part of Richmond.

We crowded into that small space all summer, sleeping in a row on the living room floor. There was a couple who lived in the apartment above my sister's, and we could hear him beating on her all the time. The reality of domestic violence was never far from us.

It took him a while to figure out where we'd gone, but my father stalked us all summer, popping up on the rare occasions we went out and telling anyone who would listen how he was going to either win Carolyn back or kill the whole family. There was a day when my mother and my siblings and I were all in my sister's yellow AMC Javelin in the supermarket parking lot. I was in the front seat, because we were trying to keep my mom hidden in the back. We thought that if he didn't see her, he would leave us alone. We were wrong.

Someone knocked on the passenger side window, and I turned to find my father standing there with a gun pointed at the window . . . at me. He demanded that my mother get out of the car to talk to him. Cassandra, tired of his antics, called his bluff and drove away. He was still shouting, but I don't think anyone inside the car ever said a word.

I spent that whole summer looking over my shoulder, always afraid. For years after that, at least once a day I'd close my eyes and see my mother, beaten and bleeding, or my father's face behind that gun pointed at my head.

Toward the end of that violent and terrifying summer, my youngest sister, Ros, needed knee surgery that couldn't be delayed any longer. We tried to keep it quiet, but my father found out about it somehow, and he came to the hospital to find us in the waiting room. He tried to pull my mother aside—he still thought she would eventually come back to him—and when she once again said no, he lost his mind and started beating her right there in the hospital hallway, outside the operating room.

We jumped in to protect her, and the doctors and nurses came running, but my father just fought all of us. In the middle of the brawl, he hit me in the nose so hard he broke it.

The blessing, if there was one, was that we were already at the hospital. The emergency medical staff saw my blood and took me straight to a different operating room to fix my nose. The doctor who did my surgery told my mother later that my father hit me so hard the bone was pushed back up into my head, and if it had gone a centimeter farther, I wouldn't be here. I still have the scar.

∞

There were no legal repercussions for my father's actions. As I said, it was a different time. But after he lost control in front of so many witnesses, the police finally persuaded him to leave our Easter Hill house and move in with his girlfriend. It was time, they said, for everyone to get on with their lives.

My mother's prayer had always been that we would make it back home before school started, because she wanted us to have a smooth education, with as few distractions as possible. And after that long, long summer of 1975, we moved back home exactly one week before the new school year started.

But when we walked in the front door, there was nothing. My father was mean, and he was bitter, and when he left, he took everything with him. And I mean *everything*. He took every last piece of furniture, every dish from the kitchen, and every towel from the closet. He even burned some of our clothes in the backyard and left the ashes for us to find. The only exception was that he left a single mattress for my sister and me to sleep on, and he acted as if he were doing us a favor with that.

When we saw our empty house, my brother and sister and I were a mess. We were wild, running around, shouting about our missing clothes and trophies. How were we supposed to go to school the next week without clothes?

But my mother just held up her hand. "Stop. Everybody, just be quiet." We did, because we did not talk back to our mother, not ever. She paused a minute and said, "Listen. All I want is peace of mind."

And in that empty house, I felt the holy quiet, the kind of quiet that comes when all of the drama has passed away. I'll never forget that. She simply would not let adversity defeat her. Our stuff was just stuff, she said, and God would provide what we needed.

And He did. Neighbors and friends helped us fill out our back-to-school wardrobes. My father eventually brought back most of our furniture. When I showed up for my junior year the next week, everything almost seemed back to normal . . . except the big brace still covering my broken nose. There was nothing to do about that.

"You go to school and you do what you have to do," my mother told me. "You have nothing to be ashamed of."

So I walked back with my head high, as if everything were normal. I was the head cheerleader that year, and I went to practice, and I cheered in the games, all with that giant brace on my face. I don't remember exactly how I was able to breathe enough to do the routines, but I did them.

That summer, I did not let adversity defeat me, either.

∾

He might have given us our furniture back, but my father wasn't done with us. Even after we got back home, he remained a terrorizing presence in our lives.

Sometime that fall, I woke up on a Saturday morning to hear my bedroom window opening. My sister, who shared my ground-floor room, was already up and in the kitchen helping with breakfast, so I was alone when I recognized my father's leg swinging in through the window. And then I saw his hand, holding a shotgun.

"Take me to your mother," he said. "I'm tired of this. I'm going to kill everybody."

I froze. What should I do? What *could* I do? I couldn't fight him on my own, and I was scared to death. He was my father, and I had been raised to always obey his orders, no matter what. On the other hand, my mother—and maybe all of us—were seconds away from being in harm's way. I got out of bed, shaking, and walked ahead of him toward the hallway, but as I passed my mother's room, I brushed as loudly as I could against the doorway, hoping and praying the person on the other side would hear me.

I knew something my father didn't, which was that my aunt, my mother's youngest sister, was in there. She'd come from Birmingham as soon as my mother's family found out about the divorce. Until then, my mother had never told them about the violence, but now they knew, and they had stepped up to protect and defend us.

My aunt Peggy was my mother's opposite. My mom's small, maybe a bit over five feet tall, and gentle. Aunt Peggy? She was six feet tall, fearless, and regularly carried a pistol in her bra.

My father had no idea Aunt Peggy was in Richmond, let alone in this house, until she came barging out of what used to be his bedroom, pistol in hand and a whole lot of swear words in her mouth.

"Boots," she said, because my father's nickname in the South was Boots. "You're leaving."

For one of the only times I can remember, my father looked scared. All of a sudden his shotgun was on the floor, and I kicked it out of the way as Aunt Peggy marched my father down the hall, through the living room, and out the front door. My mother came out of the kitchen, but Peggy just waved her away. "Boots is leaving," she said, giving him a hard look, "and he's never coming back."

He never did.

∞

My father never came to the house again, but for the next few years, throughout my high school years, he would still pop up when we didn't expect it, in the store or at some public event, ranting and threatening. His last real effort happened at my high school graduation.

When my oldest sister graduated, I noticed that the only speakers at Kennedy High School's ceremony were white boys. I asked my mother, "Can a Black girl be a president?" She said of course they could. "You can do whatever you want to do," she told me. And so right then, I decided that a Black girl was going to be senior class president of Kennedy High School's class of 1977. I didn't know that would be the beginning of a series of "firsts" in my life.

One of the responsibilities of my office was to lead the senior class into the arena that spring for our graduation ceremony. But for whatever reason, my father had surfaced again recently, threatening everyone in his family. His anger by then seemed to be directed mostly at me, perhaps in reaction to the Aunt Peggy situation. I really don't know why. He sent a message that he planned to shoot me as I walked into the auditorium.

I knew my father was full of threats that he never acted on. This wasn't the first time he'd told me that he would kill me, or even the first time he described a specific scenario. He'd never actually tried. Yet standing in front of that door that day, waiting to lead my class, I froze. Hesitation wasn't something I usually submitted to, but what if he meant his threats this time? He was crazy. He could do something.

Once again, the police were there. The cops in our neighborhood knew our family well by then. They knew how hard my mother worked to keep her kids safe and in school. And when they heard about my father's threats, they took it on themselves to come to the ceremony and to protect me from my own father. That day as I stood just inside the door, shaking with fear, the officer at the door with me noticed.

A teacher nodded at me and smiled. "Don't be afraid. They've got this. All you need to do is lead your class in."

I remembered my mother's words "You do what you have to do," and I lifted my head and led my class in to complete our high school education. My father was nowhere in sight. And, if I do say so, it was the best, most lively graduation that Kennedy High School has ever had.

There are a lot of thoughts and opinions about police in America. As the mother of two beautiful Black men and two young women, I understand it's a complicated conversation. But I am forever grateful for the men (and they were mostly men back then) who stepped up to help my mother and her children in those difficult years. Over and over, my family and I were blessed by the commitment of police officers dedicated "to protect and to serve."

~

That was the last time I remember letting my father make me afraid. After that, I decided that he was never going to be a part of me anymore. I went to college and got on with my life.

I didn't want a relationship with him, and I never had one after that. I didn't call him. I didn't see him. The night I graduated from college, he phoned me at my mother's house and said he was waiting outside—hiding in the bushes is more like it—because he bought me a car and wanted to give it to me. I told him I didn't want it. I told him I was fine without him.

I didn't invite him to my wedding and never introduced him to my kids. But it's not true to say that he wasn't part of me. His presence influenced much of what I chose to do. I never drank a beer or smoked anything in my life, for example, not even a cigarette—not because I thought there was anything wrong with it, but because those were *his* things.

To this day, more than forty years later, I still never let anyone raise their voice to me in anger—not my husband, not my kids, and not my bosses. I'm up front about this. Kenny knows I don't like conflict, and I won't let him yell at our kids, not even in those years when they were teenagers and gave their father every reason to want to yell and scream.

I've told every person I work for that my daddy was a yeller and a violent man and that for me raised voices can turn into raised fists. I'll talk and debate issues all day long, but it can't get too lively. If the tone changes, good night, I'll hang up. I'll walk out of the room. Maybe I go a little overboard with it, maybe I'm a little too sensitive, but I need peace. My sisters are the same way.

My mother took enough for all of us.

7

Take Friends on the Road
(Round 1)

Friday, January 21, 2011

Thanks to all who are keeping the prayer chain going. Cynt and her family greatly appreciate the outpouring of support from friends, family and the community, especially as they begin a very difficult period in the path to her full recovery.

Cynt began chemo treatments Tuesday of this week. To no one's surprise, she showed up with her briefcase. But instead of her usual briefcase full of AT&T work, Cynt's briefcase is now filled with other items more suitable for the road she is travelling—her Bible and some personal "good luck" gifts from friends who have provided so much support to her. She was hooked up to the chemo pump for four hours at the Cancer Center and then spent another 48 hours on the pump at home. She has, of course, experienced a lot of side effects, as many patients do with chemo treatments. Her white blood cell count dropped this week. However, she received a shot to boost that cell count on Thursday, which apparently also has some side effects of its own. Her resolve to beat this disease and to be a testament to the Lord's goodness remains strong. She will have treatments every other week for about six months. Again, Cynt sends her love to everyone and covets your continued prayers and support.

Rob Smith

The first two weeks of January were full of preparation and appointments. Having cancer, it turns out, is a full-time job. I had a whole-body PET/CT scan, then an MRI of my liver. I had a port surgically implanted in my arm to receive the chemo drugs. I joked that I was spending all of my time taking off my clothes. In reality, I spent most of my time educating myself about colon cancer, treatments, health insurance, and a hundred other details.

The hardest thing for me in those weeks leading up to my chemo was the outpatient surgery to get my port. Dr. Tyner had warned me that it was going to leave a scar, and I was already a little put off by the scar I had from my December surgery. Now I had to mark myself because of this cancer again? Part of me thought, *Okay, let's do this.* The other part of me held back.

To tell you the truth, I was *scared.* In the rush of those weeks of research, appointments, plans, and preparation, the day I got my port was the only time I actually felt afraid for what was coming.

For one thing, I was awake for the surgery, and it hurt. For another, having something put into my body just for chemo made it very real. It was my external commitment to the fight that was coming, and as I lay there on Dr. Tyner's table, I saw my life flash before my eyes. There was no turning back now. My heart was racing.

I think Dr. Tyner saw that I was feeling more fragile than usual, and he started talking to me, probably to distract me from the giant cut he was making in my arm. He asked about work, and I started talking about all the great things happening at AT&T. By the time I finished touting all the features of the new iPhone, which we were exclusively distributing at the time, my poor surgeon found himself committed to switching all of his personal and office communication services to us from their current carrier.

His kindness that day cost him a bit.

∽

I was almost never alone in those early days. Kenny came with me to every appointment. My mom and brother flew in for extra moral and medical support. Having those sets of ears at those first meetings was critical, because there were times when I just couldn't keep taking in all of those cancer words and would zone out. I'm usually very good at paying attention and focusing on what's happening in front of me, but I would be in an exam room or an office, and the voice of the person talking would fade. All I could hear was Dr. Tyner telling me, over and over, "It's bad and it's significant."

While I was zoning out, my laid-back, go-with-the-flow, type Z husband became a man on a mission.

When I was growing up, we used to say that certain things had to be done "with the quickness," which meant in a hurry. Kenny, it seemed, wanted to handle my health business with the quickness.

One morning, when I was due at the hospital for yet another round of tests, a slushy drizzle froze the roads and made it almost impossible to see or keep a car going straight. Still, Kenny insisted he could handle it. My mom and I sat, frozen in fear, as he sped and slid dangerously fast down the almost-empty freeways. We eventually made it, and my amped-up husband jumped out of our minivan and practically ran for the door without noticing that my mom and I were still collecting our purses and heart rates. When I finally caught up with him, I called him out, reminding him that while the cancer wouldn't kill me that morning, the icy road might. We should have rescheduled for another day.

Kenny, usually so calm and relaxed, shook his head. He sounded as if he were channeling my spirit when he told me, "This is urgent. Your doctor said we don't have a day to waste. We gotta get this handled *now.*"

∞

When it came time for my chemo to start, however, Kenny was in for a surprise of his own. An hour before my appointment, the posse showed up with a fifth girlfriend in tow and announced that *they* were taking me to my appointment.

At first, my husband wasn't having it. "Did you all talk to me about this? Did you even stop to think about whether *I* want to take *my* wife to her first chemo?" he thundered. "Did you even stop to think about me when you walked into my house?"

Kenny was mad and cussing up a storm, but Yvonne, always ready to be the most dramatic one in the room, just waved him away. "We're not fooling with you today. We're taking Cynt with us, but if you want to come, too, you can meet us there. You don't fit in the van."

I should pause here to say that my friends all love my husband. They call and talk to him when I'm not home, and include him in almost everything. But my cancer was hitting everyone hard, and these were five stressed-out sisters who'd decided that the way to be involved and helpful was to be at chemo. And no, they probably hadn't stopped to consider Kenny.

I refused to get into the middle of their fight. I was the one with cancer, after all, and I told them all I didn't have the energy to be a referee. If they all kept arguing, though, we were going to be late. That's how I ended up going to the Cancer Centers of North Carolina for the first time in a two-car parade, with five wound-up women ready for a party and one husband eyeing us all in exasperation.

The staff clearly didn't know what to do with us. At first they tried to say that only one person could come back to the chemo room with me, but that didn't fly. We eventually compromised on two people at a time, one on each side of my chemo chair. Everyone else had to wait in the lobby. The session lasted four hours, so they swapped out.

∽

I'd heard from a lot of people that chemo would be a beast. I'd done my homework and read all about the side effects of exhaustion and nausea, but I dismissed it all. I was tough. I was strong. I was sure I'd been through far worse.

But I'm here to tell you: Chemo is a *beast.*

I walked into that treatment center feeling good. After four hours in the chair, hooked up to a tube that poured poison straight into my arteries, I left in a haze of exhaustion and nausea. It was all I could do to get home and crawl into bed.

While I was laid out upstairs, my girlfriends coordinated with my team at work to get an update posted to the website where I'd committed to keeping a chemo journal for friends and family around the world. It had seemed like a great idea at the time, but now it was clear that by the end of a chemo treatment, I wouldn't be able to do it myself. The initial post was constructed in love by Rob Smith, our regulatory director at AT&T. After that, I wrote my own letters, and our public relations director, Clifton Metcalf, became my tech support and proofreader.

Not only did my girlfriends oversee my communications matter, but they stayed that night to make sure my family was fed, my prescriptions were filled, and my kids got to their activities. They took my griefs as their own, as well as my joys. Even Kenny grudgingly acknowledged that they were more help than hindrance.

For years, I'd publicly advocated for the importance of asking for help when we need it, for serving one another and sharing our burdens. I'd called on these friends, and many like them, time after time in my life. But there's never been anything in my life quite like chemo to show me the true power of opening up and accepting help that's joyfully offered.

And this was only the beginning of that lesson.

8

Avoid Distractions

I met Kenny on October 15, 1975. Yes, I know the exact date. As I said, I've always had a good head for numbers.

I was fifteen years old, and we were both at a regional competition for DECA, or the Distributive Education Clubs of America, which prepared high school kids to be entrepreneurs and business leaders. Part of my mother's emphasis on education, not to mention her commitment to keeping us in safe spaces, was requiring us to be involved in extracurricular activities. School was a lot more than the seven classes that were taught every day. My siblings and I played sports, sang in choirs, and participated in anything we could.

I could see right away that Kenny was one of the very few Black kids at the event, and also that he was cute and smooth, like a little Sidney Poitier. He was from a high school in the Fresno area, about three hours away, and he was a year older than me. He already had a little following of admiring DECA students. In fact, by the time I met him, he was running for a statewide office in the organization, and he approached my sister and me to help him campaign. We did, and he won.

A few months later I saw Kenny again at the spring DECA conference in San Francisco. He was on my turf, and that year I won the big statewide competition in my category, and wouldn't you know that he arranged to be the one who gave me my trophy. I still remember his smile, just for me, as we stood on that stage. Later that summer we flew to Chicago to compete in the national DECA event. It was my first time on an airplane, and we sat together, two of the very few Black kids on that plane. We talked the whole way.

I wasn't paying serious attention to the cute boy from Fresno, though. I already had my life at Kennedy High School. This was the year after that terrible summer with my dad, and at home we were learning to live for the first time without violence. I was the head cheerleader and in the honor society. My teachers, who always embraced me all through my education, were starting to guide me toward college and scholarship opportunities. It was a truly pivotal, transformational year, and I had my hands full at home.

Oh, and I also already had a boyfriend, a football player.

But Kenny was persistent. He could see something I didn't see yet. He got my school address from one of my teachers, and he started writing me letters. All I'll say is that I saw right away this boy had a way with words. He'd call me every now and then and ask if he could drive the three hours up from Fresno with some friends to visit me in the Bay Area, but my mother was strict about her daughters spending time with boys, so I told him no.

Kenny graduated and went to college in the Central Valley of California when I was a senior in high school. We kept talking through that year, and we met up once when my sister and I had a track meet in Fresno. That was fun, but what really got my attention was when he drove all the way up to be at my high school graduation—yes, the same ceremony where my father threatened me. Kenny knew about the craziness in my family by then, and he kept coming back. He was respectful to my mother.

He wasn't my boyfriend, exactly, but we both knew we were more than just friends.

All of my hard work in school, in both my classes and my extracurriculars, paid off, and I graduated with a full-ride scholarship from a private company to the college of my choice. I chose the University of California, Berkeley, just a twenty-minute bus ride from Richmond. I wanted to be close to home. My scholarship even came with a car, which I gave to my mother to make her commutes easier. Everything seemed to be coming together for the goals that I'd been pursuing for years: get an education, get a good job, and help my mom get out of the projects. I had a plan for each of these goals, and I meant to accomplish every last one of them in that order.

∽

I'll never forget the day that summer when Kenny called and told me that—surprise!—he had filed the papers to transfer from Fresno City College to San Francisco State. Fresno was a community college with a two-year associate's program, so it was normal for kids in the Central Valley to move either north or south to pursue a four-year degree. But he made it clear that he had chosen San Francisco so that he could be closer to me. He was clearly ready to get this relationship rolling.

Me? I had other plans.

The poor boy was shocked when I told him no, him being so close wasn't going to work for me. I was starting an engineering program in a top college, I explained, and I couldn't be distracted. I had to handle my business.

"I'll call you when I graduate," I told him, and hung up.

I said this despite believing that eventually this relationship was going somewhere. I knew Kenny was a genuinely good guy. Smart, funny, respectful. His mom was part of the same kind of church my family attended, and he liked my church and spiritual side. At the same time, he came from a large, loud, extended family, and so he understood that side of me and my need for peace. I knew, even then, that we had the same values and wanted the same things out of life.

Still, this was my one shot, and I wasn't going to let myself get distracted.

Kenny still moved to San Francisco and went to college there. He stayed in touch with my mom and one of my best friends, who would tell me when they saw him. But I ran into him only once or twice in those four years. At first, he was sure I had someone else and that's why I didn't want to see him. But time passed and he didn't hear about any other guy, and finally he realized that no, I was serious about my education. I was focused.

Growing up, I'd listened when my mother told her daughters that the "serious" boyfriend stuff could fall in line later, after we got our own good educations and jobs. She told us that we could get married when we wanted to, not because we needed to. I can still hear her saying, "Focus on the future" and "Show me that report card." (Yes, I still presented her with my grades each semester while in college.)

I wasn't going to go running off across the bay to be with him when what I needed was to be in the library or in study groups. Or, as he likes to describe it, "she told me to go to hell so she could go to class."

He was right—not about the going to hell part. I was much nicer than that. But I was serious about my education. My mother had instilled in me that school was my path out of the projects, which meant for me, it was my way to help get her out of the projects, too. I wasn't about to risk that now. I was in school to get a degree and a job. There were times when other guys were hanging around near me at Berkeley, interested in some kind of relationship, but they all got the same message Kenny did: I had no time for anything that wasn't part of my plan. Especially not some of the Berkeley boys, who came from private schools and who got funny looks on their faces when they found out I lived in "the projects." There was no need for someone to like me if they couldn't handle where I lived. My education mattered more than my zip code.

Finally, graduation day came. As soon as the ceremony was over, I called Kenny. I'd been thinking about this day, and planning for this call, for at least a year, so when I say "as soon as the ceremony was over," I mean that I got my diploma at two o'clock and I was on the phone by three. "I graduated, and my mom's having a party at six. You need to be there," I told him. I was fired up, Kenny says, talking like a wild woman about how I had graduated from Berkeley with top grades, a degree in human resources management, and thirteen job offers, including a good-paying job at the phone company, which was also where his dad worked for many years and coincidentally where he also worked at the time.

In my mind, this was playing out just as it was supposed to play out. I had a degree, I could help my mom, and *now* it was time to get this relationship rolling. I was ready for the romantic stuff, and I wanted it with Kenny.

On the other end of the phone was silence.

"Are you serious?" he finally asked me. I could hear the attitude in his voice. "I haven't talked to you in almost four years, and now you call me out of nowhere and want me to come over *today*?"

"Yes!" I told him. I reminded him that I told him my plan was to call him when I graduated. That's what I was doing.

"Cynt, I'm engaged."

Oh, no, no, *no.* That was definitely not the right answer.

"I told you I'd call, and you know I'm not a liar," I told him. "You know where my mom lives. I'll see you at six." And I hung up.

❧

Kenny loved that I was a smart and driven woman, but walking away for four years had been going too far, even for him. He was hurt, and so he'd found someone else.

What that "someone else" didn't know, though, was that going all the way back to high school, Kenny had told people that I would be his wife someday. Even right after I put him on hold, he visited my mother, letting her know he was right across the bridge if she needed anything. "Cynthia doesn't want to talk to me, but I'm going to marry your daughter," he told her.

So at six o'clock on the night I graduated from Berkeley, there he was on my mother's front step, ready for the party and no longer engaged. We were married two years later, and we celebrated our twenty-seventh anniversary half a year before we sat down in Dr. Tyner's office.

I like to tease him about how close he came to missing his blessing with me, but the truth is that I've gotten my own share of blessings out of the deal. Kenny is still the smart, laid-back, funny, smooth-talking guy I met at the DECA competition all those years ago, and I'm lucky that my "no distractions" plan didn't cost me his love.

As the years passed and our family members have gone off to college—first the nieces and nephews and then our own kids— it's Kenny who never fails to ask them, as we are getting ready to leave them in their first dorm room, "You got a phone call to make?"

He keeps a straight face as he tells them, "This is the time where you call and say, 'I'll talk to you when I graduate.' Tell them they can stay in touch with us, but you cut them off right now. It's a tradition in our family."

9

Appreciate the Journey
(Round 2)

Tuesday, February 1, 2011

Hello, my friends,

Greetings from the clubhouse.

Yes, I call the Cancer Centers of North Carolina the chemo clubhouse, because I have joined a special team of people. We are fighting for our lives and winning. I have great doctors in my corner and I have the Lord in the cancer boxing ring with me. He is not on the sidelines.

I feel your prayers, love and positive vibes in the ring with me too. Thank you for EVERYTHING you have done to support me and my family on this journey. You're incredible!

I began Round 2 of chemotherapy today. Round 1 was difficult and presented some anticipated complications (extreme nausea and fatigue) and some unanticipated complications (dangerously low white blood cell count). With the assistance of a shot that had painful side effects, we were able to raise the WBC levels to the point where it looks like I will NOT need another shot this week. HALLELU-JAH! I had already decided that this baby was not getting that shot again.

I had about 9 "non-Cynt like" days and 5 good days during Round 1. I was able to go to work on January 31st and that was wonderful AT&T team therapy—just what I needed.

Please continue to pray for me and my family during Round 2. Ken Anthony is about 100 miles away in his first year of college, and for some reason now he just shows up at home unexpectedly on the weekend (highly unusual and we know why). I know my health situation is weighing heavily on his young mind so please say an extra prayer for him. Kenny and the girls amaze me every day. Shirley and Alicia were very excited when I went to work yesterday because, according to Shirley, that means "mom is not dying."

YES! That is true! By the grace of God and because of all of your prayers, I am very much alive and determined to get through 12 rounds of chemo in the clubhouse. While my mind is set on June 21–23, the last round, I am appreciating this journey each day for the blessings it brings and the many things I'm learning about the awesome God I serve.

Thanks again for your love,

Cynt

I'd been distracted by the two-car parade the first time I went to chemo, but the next time I pulled up to the Cancer Centers of North Carolina, I recognized the building. It was in the same medical complex as my primary care doctor, and I'd driven past the sign dozens of times in the previous years, whenever I was pulling into the driveway. I'd always say a prayer for the people in there, but I'd certainly never gone inside myself to see if I could help. To be honest, I'd see "cancer" on the sign and feel grateful that I wasn't there.

Now I wasn't passing by. Now *I* was the one in the building, and I sure hoped someone driving by was praying for me, because chemo was brutal in ways I never expected.

There were things about chemo that I just never anticipated, like the terrible shots the nurses gave me if my pre-chemo blood work showed that I didn't have enough white blood cells to effectively fight off infections. Both my cancer and my chemo drugs caused the number of white blood cells in my bone marrow to drop dangerously low. But those shots . . . the pain was so deep in my bones that after that first shot I couldn't even sit down. My tailbone and back hurt like no pain I'd ever felt before, not even when I was in labor. I swear I could feel my body making every individual infection-fighting white blood cell.

And then there was the fatigue. When a former colleague who'd been through his own stage 3 colon cancer heard about my diagnosis, he called to offer some unsolicited but generous advice. I listened, I confess, with some skepticism.

Gary told me that I was about to experience fatigue as I'd never felt it before, and when it happened (not *if,* but *when*), I should immediately yield. He said he knew I thought I was Superwoman, but I wasn't going to be able to push through it, so I should put myself to bed and wait it out.

I was polite on the outside, but inside I was thinking, "Sure, Gary. I'm a working mom. I've been tired before. I can power through."

Then I started chemo, and not long after round 2 I felt a wave of exhaustion that was like nothing I'd ever felt before. I remembered what Gary said, and I told Kenny, "I need you to help me up the stairs, because I'm going to bed." And I did. Thank God I'd been warned and didn't try to power through the feeling. What would have happened if I had tried to drive to the grocery store or keep up with a work meeting like that? What would I have done if Gary hadn't offered his wisdom and experience?

❧

Despite the waves of fatigue, I still tried to believe that chemo would not disrupt my work schedule. *How little I knew what was coming.*

Dr. Tyner and Dr. Eisenbeis both warned me that it would be difficult if not impossible to work while I was getting chemo. They had also explained the fatigue that would get worse with each round and would change day by day. Dr. Eisenbeis told me to expect more "not so good" days than "good" ones.

Still, I had projects underway, and I was determined to see them through. How bad could "not so good" really be? I figured I would get ahead on the "good" days and everything would be fine.

In those early weeks before my first chemo appointment, I had flooded my boss, and then his boss, with so many long emails about that audit and other matters that were still ongoing that they had to tell me to focus on my health plan. Well, actually, what David said, politely but firmly, was that he didn't want to see another work message from me for at least a week. He seemed to understand what I denied: Beating cancer was going to be my new full-time job. My old routine didn't exist anymore, even if I wasn't ready to see it.

Meanwhile, my friends and colleagues at AT&T were coming to terms with the fact that I was engaged in the fight for my life as well. My favorite story is from my friend Sylvia Russell, who at the time was the president of AT&T Georgia. When our boss told the team about my cancer, Sylvia was devastated. Unable to work, she went to the grocery store with the idea that she would cook a pot roast to calm her nerves. The problem was that Sylvia had never made a pot roast in her life. In fact, much like me, Sylvia was not often found in a kitchen. Her assistant had to talk her through a grocery list while she walked around the store in a daze.

As much as my colleagues grieved with me, they also became protective of me. Sylvia, in particular, found a response that was more in line with her calling than a pot roast. When I started chemo, she volunteered to temporarily fill in for me at work while I was out handling my medical business.

I tried to argue and told her I didn't need anybody doing my job. But oh so sweetly, in a way you'd think only a Southerner could, Sylvia told me that she wasn't doing my job. She already had her own job. But she knew the ropes and most of the players involved with my job. She explained she was just coming in as backup so that I wouldn't worry about anyone *else* sabotaging me or trying to use my illness to advance their own career. She reminded me that because I trusted her—and I did—I would know that I could work whenever I could but also step away to fight cancer when I needed to. We would make those decisions on a day-by-day basis. She promised to always keep me informed and made it abundantly clear that I was still in charge.

Sylvia was exactly what I needed, even when I didn't know I needed it. She understood that I wanted to work. I wanted to take every call and personally be there for every meeting. And at first, I really tried. Sylvia would sit silently on phone calls to our legislators and stakeholders while I worked on our agenda. She took notes and stayed informed without ever overstepping.

Finally, one day on a regular weekly conference call, I was so exhausted I couldn't keep up. I was well into my "not so good" days of fatigue and nausea. I'd been pushing and pushing, and I just couldn't anymore. I knew Sylvia was on the call, ready to step in and keep the work moving smoothly forward, so I hung up. And it was such a beautiful thing, and such a gift of service, that I skipped every conference call after that until I was done with chemo.

∞

Stepping away from my daily work routine was hard for me, but to my surprise it was even harder for my daughter.

Shirley continued to struggle with my illness. My feisty, emotionally charged, dramatic daughter had finally stopped talking about that Julia Roberts movie, but she was still convinced I was dying, and she offered her opinion to anyone who would listen. That got my attention, because Shirley wasn't typically so vocal with her opinions. Finally, I sat her down and asked her why she still thought I was going to die, even though I was getting treatment.

"Because things aren't normal," she said. According to her, only imminent death would keep me away from working late nights at the office. "I'll know that everything's okay again when I see your work outfit hanging on the closet door at night, and the next morning you're wearing that outfit when you kiss me to wake me up, and you make us all breakfast before you go to work, and then you come home when it's dark."

My girl is observant. She was right: I'd been getting my work clothes ready every night for as long as Shirley could remember. For that matter, I'd been getting my clothes out every night ever since I was a little girl. That was my mother's routine that I'd carried forward. Always move forward. Always look ahead. And I worked late into the evening a lot, especially since we'd come to North Carolina and the kids were older. Shirley wasn't used to me being home before dinner, and now I was home all the time, wearing sweats and sleeping through her morning routine.

It was an aha mama moment to realize that my daily routine had become Shirley's stability, and at sixteen my baby needed stability.

That night I told Kenny I needed to kick back into a normal routine for a day, even if that's what ended up killing me. I got a work outfit together, ironed it, and hung it on my closet door. Then I called Shirley to our bedroom on some excuse so that she'd see it. I pretended not to notice when her eyes brightened a little.

The kiss and breakfast the next morning required effort. The chemo fatigue was strong, and the walk to her bedroom felt as if it were a mile. Making breakfast, even if it was just sticking some Pop-Tarts in the toaster, was even harder. The drive was excruciating, and possibly dangerous. But I was doing it for my daughter.

By mid-morning I made it out the door and to the AT&T building. Then, out of my daughter's concerned sight, I took a long nap at the office. I woke up with a bit of a second wind and actually got a little bit of work done, then made sure not to come home until the normal time, long after the kids were home from their after-school practices and rehearsals.

Shirley met me at the garage door. "Mom's not going to die!" she shouted back to the family. "She's just having a midlife crisis!" She turned a corner that night and never mentioned me dying again.

After that, I continued to hang an outfit on the closet door every night, even when the chemo fatigue was high and I didn't wear it the next day. And when I did go to the office or a work event, I made sure not to get home too early—even if it meant that I needed to rest somewhere else midday. If my mother could make it to my brother's high school graduation after what she endured that infamous day in 1975, I could certainly drag myself to the office and give Shirley the stability she needed to keep going with her little life.

10

Serving Others

"Everybody can be great," said Dr. Martin Luther King, Jr., "be-cause anybody can serve."

When my parents lived in Birmingham, my mother and her family often attended the 16th Street Baptist Church, where Dr. King was a regular guest, and his ideas and teaching continued to be a big part of all of our lives long after we moved, especially his ideas about service.

When we weren't at church or at school, my brothers and sisters and I visited residents who lived in a convalescent hospital, cleaned the Boys & Girls Clubs, worked in soup kitchens, and cleaned parks. My mother's lesson was clear: However poor we were, or however troubled things might be at home, we had a responsibil-ity to what Dr. King called "vigorous and positive action."

No matter what was happening at home, she showed us the importance of carrying on and engaging the world with grace and with grit. There was so much that she could have been bitter about, and so much that she could have used as an excuse, but she never did. She gathered herself every day and went into a world that eyed her skin color and her home address with suspicion, and she showed her children that it was our responsibility to make that world better.

By the time I went to college, service was so ingrained in me that in my first year as a Delta Gamma, I was named the vice president of philanthropy. The sorority's motto to "do good" is what drew me to them in the first place, and I guess it's what drew them to me, too. I was the only Black woman in a sea of 110 primarily white sorority sisters, but they offered me not only the hand of friendship but also the honor of being an officer and guiding their important efforts to reach out.

Then, when I weighed my career options after college, I had two priorities: I wanted to make as much money as possible, and I wanted to be a boss. Money was what would help get us out of the projects, but being a boss would give me the chance to impact others. I was a people person and called to serve. It wasn't the easiest path, but I wasn't trying to do what was easy. I was trying to do what was right for me.

∽

Pacific Telephone and Telegraph made me the best offer; as I remember, they beat out the competition by just six hundred dollars a year, and the runner-up was the company that gave me my scholarship. But hey, I said I wanted the most money, and Pacific Telephone delivered. I said I wanted to lead, and just a couple of weeks out of college it made me a shift supervisor in charge of a roomful of operators and part of a management fast-track program that offered mentoring and a commitment to advancement.

That's not to say the road was always smooth for a Black girl making her way in 1981 corporate America.

My very first week of work, my boss's boss pulled me aside and told me I couldn't wear my shoes—my *only* pair of dress shoes, mind you, because I was still waiting for my first paycheck—to work anymore, because red wasn't an "appropriate" color for the workplace. She gave me the impression only streetwalkers wore red heels like mine.

"And your braids have to come out tonight," she told me, looking at my hair with distaste. She said it made her uncomfortable to be in a meeting with someone who looked the way I did. I was too "ethnic."

Yes, that was her word, but I didn't take offense. In fact, in that moment I was grateful, thinking that this woman was looking out for me and helping me advance. I went home and told my mother that we had to take all of my braids out right away. If you know anything about braids, you know they take a long time to put in and an even longer time to take out. My mother, my sister, and I were up all night, undoing those braids. I went back to the office the next day with straight hair, wearing some black shoes and a blue suit my sister lent me.

That conservative, all-business style became my primary workplace look for the next nineteen years. For the most part, I kept my big hats and bright colors separate; those were my church clothes. I didn't think much about why. I didn't consider speaking up. I wasn't there to look a certain way, anyway. I was there for the people.

∾

In my forty-plus years of work, I've learned that to be a good leader, I need to spend at least half of my working hours investing in the people around me: listening, learning, and loving them. It doesn't matter whether they're telephone operators or NBA superstars, and it doesn't matter what my title is, either. I know that I was put on this earth to serve others. I chose to work in corporate America in order to make work life better for the greatest number of employees possible and to enable their nonwork life by making sure they can feed their kids, take care of their elderly parents, send their kids to college, and do whatever they need to do. If that means I take paperwork home and do it after my own kids are in bed, so be it. If it means I have worked seven days a week for most of my career, that's all right. I knew early in my career that my calling was to serve in the workplace, so it never felt as if I were giving up a lot of personal time. It felt as though I was privileged to answer a unique calling to serve in a way that I could.

And if serving the people on my team means learning how to climb telephone poles, then that's what I'll do.

Back in the early 1990s, I was a district manager overseeing several departments, including the on-the-ground telephone pole repair crews. I was told that I was the second woman to have my job, and the first Black person to have my job, so it was triply important that I knew what I was talking about when I represented the people who reported to me. I wanted to understand what my team experienced. What did they go through?

When one of the union representatives mentioned that the crews all had to go to "pole-climbing school," I told him to sign me up.

He laughed at me. "District managers don't go to pole-climbing school."

"Well, I do," I said. How could I lead someone if I wasn't willing to step into their job? How else was I going to know what this team needed?

So I went to pole-climbing school. Somewhere in a closet I still have the boots and belt I wore on my last day of training, when I had to climb more than thirty feet up a pole and hang a drop. The union reps and all of the techs were incredulous that a "suit" would be getting her hands dirty. They came and cheered for me, and it smoothed our relationship for years to come.

But I didn't go to pole-climbing school just to get ahead. Sure, it helped. Kenny and I helped my mom get out of Easter Hill soon after I started working, and in the time since we've been able to support dozens of programs, mostly those that help kids who need stable homes, education, and a shot at life. The Bible says that to whom much is given, much will be required. Well, the Lord has given me a lot of blessings, and it's my opinion that my job is to find the best ways to give those things back. Kenny likes to joke that he's going to die a poor man, because as much as I bring home, I give just as much away. I tell him that he's wrong, because he'll die rich in spirit. I might give away all of our stuff, but I promise I'll leave him his spirit.

But it's not the money that keeps me in my office late every night. It's the chance to touch lives, and to allow others to touch my life.

I work long hours because I take the time to invest in the people around me. My meetings run long because we're all chitchatting about our families, and then my paperwork has to get done at night, and that's great, too. It's the people who matter most.

I often think of the time when I was told that one of my direct reports, Linda, was going to be laid off as part of a restructuring. Linda had been with the company for twenty years, and everything in me knew that letting her go was a mistake. She had seniority, experience, and the skills to help the team move forward. Still, I was told that her name was on "the list," and she had to go. I was supposed to deliver the news and instruct her to pack her office the same day.

Well, that wasn't going to work. After expressing why I thought this was wrong, I informed my bosses that if they made me lay off Linda, then two people would be leaving the building that day, because I was going, too. I called Kenny and told him that I couldn't work for a company that would treat anyone in such an unfair manner, and then I called the CEO of the company and told him the same thing.

I started packing my office and taking boxes to my car. On one of my trips back inside, my assistant called me to the phone. One of my dear colleagues in Washington, D.C., told me that Linda's employment was safe. She would stay with the company and work on my colleague's team, effective immediately. She was happy about it. Linda was happy about it. Eventually, even my boss's boss called to commend me for taking a stand. I was happy that they did right by Linda.

I went out to my car and brought the boxes back to my office, ready to continue to work for the people around me.

∽

The more I served, the more my teams produced. I'd worked on merger teams and helped transition half a dozen new companies into the business, navigated multiple company name changes linked to the acquisitions, and most important, supported the overall business shift from "the phone company" to a technology and entertainment company. The more my teams produced, the more promotions I got—from supervisor to manager, manager to director, director to vice president, vice president to senior vice president, and finally, three years before my diagnosis, to the position of president of AT&T North Carolina.

Every time I saw that title, I remembered the summer that my parents finally divorced, when my father told my younger sister, Ros, and I that we would be nothing without him. "You'll be hookers on the street," is what he actually said. Those terrible words echoed in my head for years. They made me cry many times. Sometimes I would just stare into space while his hurtful false prophecy pressed down on my spirit.

But that all happened later. In the moment, facing his anger and my sister's devastation, I handled it. At all of fifteen years old, I told Ros no, our father's words weren't true. Instead, we were going to be the first people in our family to graduate from a big college. (We were.) We were going to help our mom get out of Easter Hill. (We did, although my mother worked so hard that given time she would have gotten herself out without us.) And, I told her, someday I was going to be the president of something.

And here I was.

Yes, Dad, I was making my money on the street. But it was Wall Street.

Hallelujah.

11

Take Nothing for Granted
(Round 3)

Tuesday, February 15, 2011

Dear friends,

Round 3 in the Clubhouse began today. It is amazing how the Lord works! In just the past few days, he put three different people in my path, all of whom encouraged me and shared that staying well hydrated and active helps the chemo meds work through the system. So Winston and I will be moving around more. (I named my chemo pump Winston. I'll explain that sometime, but many of the ladies will already understand.)

Round 2 had its challenges, but it also had some positives, such as the additional medications that helped with the nausea. Remember I said I wouldn't take another shot to boost the white blood cell count? Well, the Lord reminded me that I'm not in control—it looks like I will have another one on Thursday. The side effects of the shot are painful and I really did not want to do it. But I prayed for the Lord to give me the wisdom to make the right decision. I'm not big on drugs, but I'm not big on pain either! This time I'm going to start taking the pain pills when they give them to me and see if I can get ahead of it. We're working toward finishing Round 12 (the last one!) on June 23rd. So, I'm on a mission here. I'm not going to tolerate delays. Whatever I need to do to keep on track, that's what we will do.

Over the past couple of weeks, the Lord has shown me a wonderful lesson about all the things I've taken for granted for so long. I'm keeping a list and will share it sometime, but it will include things like taste buds, energy, and being able to swallow a cold beverage or stand barefoot on a cold hardwood floor. And I am learning to appreciate time with my family so much more.

Speaking of family, Kenny and the kids are doing great. Your extra prayers for them were answered. Anyway, I know I will be much more grateful for life's everyday blessings after I've come through this. The fact that there is nothing negative in my spirit has a lot to do with the hundreds of cards, calls and posts on the CaringBridge site. I read everything—usually two or three times—and it always gives me a lift. A card, a page of bible verses or a pair of warm socks like those a friend in Washington DC sent me, may seem like small things. But those gestures mean so much to me and I appreciate them. Most of all, thank you for your prayers. I love you!

Cynt

We were settling into a new routine that started when I spent four hours in the chemo chair every other Tuesday, with an IV plugged into the port in my left arm.

My time "in the chair" was precious to me. While there's a lot about chemo that's awful, I remember those hours at the Clubhouse as some of the best parts of my week, because those were the hours I knew I was fighting back, killing the bad cells and reclaiming my life. It was also the time that I felt the most "Cynt-like."

My life had taken on a new rhythm. Where once I lived week to week, planning around church on Sunday and my weekday work responsibilities, now I lived by my fourteen-day chemo cycle, which consistently became nine "bad" days, filled with exhaustion and pain, followed by five good ones after the chemo drugs had mostly worked their way out of my system. My day in the chair was the last of my good days. It was a chance to talk to my buddies, listen to my music, and make work calls I knew I wouldn't have the energy for in the coming week.

I brought a call list to every round of chemo, and it usually included a few influential and important people who could help with our AT&T agenda. When I talked to someone, I wasn't shy about letting them know where I was calling from; I'd sometimes maybe even hold the phone up right next to the machine while I adjusted the tubes so they could hear the whir and noise of it. I'd remind the person on the other end that the physical effects of chemo might kick in any minute, and so I had to be quick, while I still had the strength to talk.

At one point, the then-governor of North Carolina, Bev Perdue, caught on to my ploy for sympathy. "Why do you always call me from the chemo chair?" she asked me. "How am I supposed to tell you no?"

❧

When I got up from that chemo chair, I wasn't done with my treatment. The medical staff would unhook me from the big chemo pump and immediately attach a smaller, portable pump, which continued to drip chemo medicine into my bloodstream for forty-eight more hours.

I had to carry that pump everywhere with me. I even had to sleep with it, much to Kenny's annoyance. "It's noisy," he complained.

"He's saving my life," I told him. "He's giving me my groove back."

And that's why I named that little pump Winston, after Taye Diggs's character in the movie *How Stella Got Her Groove Back*. Some of you may be too young to remember that one, but the basic story is that Angela Bassett plays a successful single mom in her forties who works too much and never has fun until she meets Winston, a *much* younger man who brings sparks back into her life.

Cancer was sucking up a lot of my spark and my groove, and Winston was my answer to getting my life back. I showed my chemo pump some love so that he would show me some love in return. I decorated Winston for various holidays and put him in a little bathrobe at night to match my pajamas. *Do your thing, baby!*

Because Winston was my constant companion, and because I was still going to live as much of my life as I could, I also took him with me when I went to meet with policy makers or other influencers on behalf of AT&T. I wasn't shy about milking my chemo for anything that would benefit others. I decided to use cancer instead of letting it use me, and to get something from this awful disease that had interrupted my life. I even showed up on the floor of the North Carolina legislature with my chemo pump on my hip. Rumor has it one representative told someone, "Just give her whatever she wants so that she goes home. She really looks like she needs to lie down."

I was there to finish the job, no matter what.

≈

To that representative's credit, I probably did need to lie down. After four hours in the chair, I would tell the nurses I was "going under," and it was no joke. I would go home and crawl into bed.

Wednesday would be horrible. Thursday would be worse. I could barely function with all that poison flowing into me. The weakness, nausea, and back pain felt as if they might kill me if the cancer didn't. On those "nine bad days," I often couldn't eat. Kenny would have to make sure I was in our bedroom with the door closed before he and the kids ate dinner, because even the smell of food would make me sick. Everything about me felt muted; even my voice was barely more than a whisper. It felt as though I were living in someone else's body.

After a few rounds of chemo, I started to adjust to the ups and downs of the fourteen-day schedule. I tried not to talk to many people during the bad days, because I didn't want them feeling sorry for me. But one week I happened to be awake and near the house phone when it rang. Without thinking, I answered it. When I heard my niece Gynelle's voice, I knew I'd made a mistake.

Gynelle is the daughter of my oldest sister, the first grandchild, and she's named after me. (My middle name is Gynelle.) When she was little, Kenny and I would take care of her every weekend, from Friday to Sunday. We were close.

She was an adult now, and I knew she and her husband, Ben, were regularly fasting and praying for me while I went through my treatments. In fact, she'd called that day to talk to her uncle Kenny to see how things were going. But when she heard my faint and fake "Hey, Doo," her own voice got shaky.

We kept the conversation brief, and as soon as I hung up, I went back to sleep.

About a week later, my doorbell rang late at night. I was well into my five good days by then and feeling very "Cynt-like." When I heard the bell, I jumped up and went to the top of the staircase, where I could see the door. Kenny was downstairs and would answer it, I knew, but he was taking his time getting there.

The doorbell rang again, and I yelled, "Who is it?" I didn't hear the answer, so I yelled again, loud enough to wake up Shirley and Alicia, who joined me on the steps, ready to challenge whoever was trying to invade our space so late at night.

Kenny finally made it to the door and opened it, and I was stunned to see my sister Cassandra and her best friend, Corlis, standing there. My sister looked equally stunned to see me.

I realized right away what had happened.

Gynelle had called her mother in tears after we hung up, and that set off a chain of family conversations. It was hard for my mother and sisters to be so far away from me during this time. They'd been counting on Kenny and the kids to tell them what I needed, but now, according to Gynelle, maybe we were holding out on them. Maybe I was in much worse shape than they imagined.

After much back-and-forth among my siblings and extended family, it was decided that my oldest sister, Gynelle's mother, Cassandra, was physically closest to us, and so she needed to drive out to our house from where she lived in St. Louis to get a face-to-face read on the situation. Of course, no one bothered to tell me about the plan, because they were convinced I was dying.

Cassandra and Corlis had driven more than thirteen hours that day, thinking the whole time they would find me on my deathbed. Instead, they saw two sleepy teenagers and a strong, fit, and vibrant mother.

"Hey, woman," I said in my normal, loud voice.

Cassandra managed to say, "Is this what cancer looks like? You're not even sick!"

"Come in and close the door," I told her. "Find a bedroom, and we'll go shopping tomorrow. And tell Gynelle I'm okay. She just caught me on day two."

I'd been trying to protect my family from having to see me at my "cancer worst," but Cassandra's visit was a blessing. Once she was assured that my "good" days were as normal as my "bad" ones, we talked a lot during her visit about things we all took for granted and how important it was to readjust when 64 percent of my days were "bad." While I had previously taken for granted that I'd have the same energy and routine every day, now I started to appreciate and embrace the irregularity of the new routine and stopped trying to protect the people closest to me from my reality.

12

When Life Doesn't Follow the Plan

When Kenny and I got married, my plan was to work for two years and then get pregnant and give birth to our first child. We'd both come from big families with lots of siblings, and we always agreed we wanted a houseful of kids. I pictured four or five boys.

I thought that starting a family would be like all of my other goals. I would make a plan and make it happen.

Sometimes, though, the Lord has other plans.

First, I got pregnant right after our wedding. That was okay. It sped up my time line, but I was excited to start our family. I still have a picture of me sitting outside on a sunny day in a cute white maternity sundress, twenty-three years old and just starting to show. Kenny had asked me to come with him while he went fishing, and I was just enjoying the day in the sun. You can see the glow coming off me, because I was already so in love with our baby.

A couple of days later, though, everything went south. I was sixteen and a half weeks pregnant and an engineer at Pacific Bell, working at a desk in a roomful of men. My back had been bothering me all day, but I hadn't been paying attention until suddenly my cute striped maternity dress felt wet and there was a puddle of water under my chair. I had no idea what was happening. It didn't even occur to me for a second that my bag of waters could break that early.

One of my colleagues saw my expression and asked if I was okay. Florian told me later that something about the way I was walking and moving that day hadn't seemed right, so he and one of our assistants had been keeping a concerned eye on me. When I whispered, "I'm all wet," they knew not only what that meant but also how dangerous it was.

"Honey," the assistant said, "I think you're in labor." There were tears in her eyes.

Within minutes they had an ambulance on its way, and someone had called Kenny. Florian had even found a blanket to wrap around me so that I wouldn't be embarrassed by my wet dress when we had to take the elevator down to the lobby. There was nothing that could hide my tears, though.

"What does this mean?" I kept asking. "It's too soon for this baby."

Kenny met me at the hospital, where a doctor who lacked any kind of bedside manner explained in very clinical terms that I was in preterm labor and it was far enough along that it couldn't be stopped. While Kenny and I just stared at him in shock, he went on to tell us I would need to labor all the way to delivery, even though the baby I carried would be too premature to survive more than a minute or two.

That was *definitely* not part of my plan. Losing a baby was a flat-out nightmare.

It was hard enough to accept that I would lose this child, but to go through labor and delivery first was devastating. It didn't help that the nurses kept coming at me with questions no grieving mother should have to consider. Did I want them to put the baby on my chest until he passed? Did I want a death certificate? Did I want imprints of the baby's footprints? (The answers, for me, were all no, though due to an administrative error it all ended up happening anyway.)

The hours passed. I wept all the way through my labor, knowing that I was going through the pain for nothing. And that labor took its time, let me tell you. After a full day of tears and contractions, they finally wheeled me into the delivery room . . . and that's when Kenny fainted.

I still like to remember Kenny all laid out on the floor, because in that whole long, dark day it was the only thing that made me crack a smile. He told me later that the bright lights and sterile medical equipment reminded him of mechanics working on a car. Then there was all of the blood—I was hemorrhaging pretty badly—and one minute he was standing there, holding my hand and thinking, "This is my wife, not a car," and the next thing he knew, my hand was gone and he was on the floor. I could see the nurses trying not to laugh behind their masks as they got him awake and back up, and he came back to my bedside . . . and then he fainted again.

This time, I told the staff to send Kenny out to the hallway and get my mama from the waiting room to come in with me. She'd done this six times before. She could handle a little blood.

They brought Kenny back into the room just before I gave birth to a tiny baby boy. As we'd been told to expect, he was too premature to survive.

The next few days were a mess of physical and emotional pain. My breasts swelled with milk I couldn't give to my child. Friends and family members tried to help, but too often ended up saying things we didn't need to hear. Kenny actually had to send his parents back home to Fresno when his father—a good man, but sometimes socially inept—asked what kind of wife I was if I couldn't give my husband a child.

I was filled with grief, physically and emotionally devastated. But underneath all of that, I was simply perplexed. *What had hap-*

pened? What had gone wrong? I'd been planning for this baby for months, dreaming of starting a family for my whole life. How did it not happen? I pestered the doctors and read everything I could, educating myself. I just needed more data so I could make a better plan.

Underneath all of that, of course, was the uncomfortable truth that I wasn't yet ready to wrestle with: My miscarriage was the first time that I'd made a major plan that had totally fallen apart. It was the first time in a long time that something so important was so out of my control.

I should have stopped, prayed, and listened to the Lord about the experience. I should have asked what He had in mind.

Instead, I doubled down. I wanted a baby even more.

All of the people around us—our families and our friends in church—were having babies. My colleagues' wives were having babies. If they could do it, I told Kenny, so could I. I decided that we would try again as soon as possible.

A year later, with my doctor's blessing, I was pregnant again. At sixteen and a half weeks, I miscarried another boy.

A year after that, it happened a third time, right at sixteen and a half weeks.

I went to all of the doctors, but no one could tell us why it was happening. All of the genetic and physical tests were inconclusive. We knew that with every pregnancy, I'd suffered something called hyperemesis gravidarum, which is the fancy term for severe nausea. To put it bluntly, I threw up *all the time.* I was constantly dehydrated and malnourished, losing weight even as the baby inside me grew. Did that prevent my body from carrying a baby? One test revealed a septum in my uterus, which might wedge a growing baby into an awkward shape. Was that sending me into preterm labor? I had surgery to fix that.

After my third miscarriage, Kenny came to me with his concerns. He didn't want to try again. "I didn't marry you for your ability to have kids," he told me more than once. "We can grow our family in other ways. We can adopt. We can be the best uncle and auntie. We don't have to do this."

But I *did* have to do it. I needed to stick to the plan. I waved him off and told him I wouldn't give up.

But sixteen and a half weeks after I got pregnant a fourth time, I miscarried again, and that fourth miscarriage almost killed me. I had bled every time I went into labor, but this time it was so bad that a doctor came to Kenny and told him I needed immediate, emergency surgery to stop the hemorrhaging. It was bad enough that he asked my husband, if something happened in the operating room, should the medical team focus on saving me or the baby?

Kenny's still mad about that. Everything we'd been through, and everything we'd seen, just all came out in a rush on that poor doctor, and I heard later from the nurses how my husband *explained* just how stupid he thought that question was. "Save my wife, of course."

I came through the surgery just fine, but Kenny never really got over it. "This is crazy," he told me, when I started to talk about getting pregnant again. "This makes no sense. You come close to death *every time* you get pregnant. This needs to come to an end."

I tried to brush him off, the way I'd done before. "I want to have a baby, and I'm the one taking on all the pressure and stress."

Kenny pushed back. "No, you're not the only one with pressure. *You're* not in the position of watching *me* almost die every few years." He looked at me hard. "I don't ever—*ever*—want to have a doctor ask me about saving your life again. I'm tired of this. You need to stop."

Looking back, I know that he said "you need to stop," not "we need to stop." He had stopped a long time ago. This was just me and my determination to make life fit to my plans.

I heard Kenny out that day. I knew having a baby and raising a child involved both of us, and the father of my children deserved some say in the decision. But I still held on to my dream of having a baby.

We waited for three years, and we agreed to try one final time. We'd take all the precautions, pull out all the stops. But this was it. I had one last chance.

13

Make a Grand Entrance (Round 4)

Wednesday, March 2, 2011

Greetings from the Chemo Clubhouse, where the Lord is still in charge and working miracles daily! I entered the Clubhouse yesterday morning in pearls, sweats, a hairdo that's starting to shed, and fluffy socks! :-)

I am excited to begin Round 4, as we are one-third of the way into my treatment plan. We are making great progress and continue to be encouraged by your love and thoughtfulness and by the scripture that so many of you have shared: "For I know the plans I have for you, declares the Lord, plans to prosper you and not harm you, plans to give you hope and a future" (Jeremiah 29:11). I am quite hopeful and I've claimed a disease free, healthy future with a brand new ATTitude. For the present, I'm thankful each day, whether it's one of my 9 "whose body is this?" days or one of my 5 "feeling more like Cynt" days. Because of you, I'm celebrating life EVERY DAY.

Over the past two weeks I've experienced the normal chemo side effects and gained a new understanding of "I can feel it in my bones," since the side effect of the White Blood Cell booster shot is a great deal of pain. I'm determined to endure these shots as often as necessary and—praise the Lord!—it has paid off. My WBC count was up but my platelets were dangerously low. So, we made some adjustments to the chemo meds for this round to hopefully address the low platelet count and were able to tip-off March Madness in the Clubhouse on schedule.

I've begun planning a St. Patrick's Day celebration and a College Basketball day in the clubhouse. Hopefully the colors blue and gold will make it into the NCAA tournaments (Go Bears!) and provide colorful cheer. If not, there are two other shades of blue (Carolina blue and Duke blue) that I'm sure will delight the patients and staff. They are all excited about the March party plans.

I went into the office on Monday. As I was driving home, I got caught up in the wicked thunderstorm that swept through the Triangle. It was pouring rain, lightning was flashing and I was gripping the steering wheel and praying. By the time I safely made it home, the Lord had helped me understand that a virtual thunderstorm swept into my life on December 15, 2010, my 51st birthday. Since then, I have experienced sadness, worry, weakness, and anxiety. But I have also experienced peace, comfort and an incredible outpouring of love. And through it all, I've never doubted that this thunderstorm is heaven-sent for a Divine purpose. I remain optimistic and am hanging on tightly to God's promises. "We" are beating cancer! (We've actually already beaten it; we're just taking some extra steps to keep it in my past.)

Please continue to pray for all of the Marshalls. My prayers for this chemo round are to (1) be able to eat more and not lose too many more pounds (I need my hips), (2) avoid the flu and seasonal illnesses, and (3) keep the kids focused on handling their school business. I'm really proud of them! Thanks for your prayers, encouragement and love. I love you back and I am praying for all of you and your families as we continue this journey together!

Cynt

Being the fashionista that I am, I sashayed into the cancer center for every session with a whole color scheme, nice shoes, and—of course—my pearls. They were a gift from my friend Patty when I started chemo, and I wore them all the time, even with my sweats, because they made me feel good at times when I felt awful. To this day, I wear pearls whenever I'm facing a crisis.

By my fourth visit, I recognized the "chemo smell" that met me at the door and filled the building. I knew the nurses and where their stations were, and checked in with them and with Dr. Eisenbeis. I had my blood drawn to check those pesky white blood cell numbers.

"How are you doing today?" my favorite nurse asked me.

I told her the truth: I was doing great at that moment. But then I smiled ever so sweetly and reminded her, "But y'all are going to take care of that any minute. I know you're about to bring me down."

We laughed, but we both knew it was true. There was nothing that could change the nine days of exhaustion and pain that were coming, and I didn't blame her for them. But knowing it made me even more determined that these last hours of my "good" days be fun.

∽

When my name was called, I made my way down the hall to the infusion suite, where the real action was. It was a big room with about fifteen or so recliners lined up along the walls, which in some strange way always reminded me of a hair salon, only instead of bowls of warm water and trays of beauty products, there were humming machines and IV needles. Each chemo chair had a table, and a chair for the patient's support person, or in my case two chairs.

My friends Hokey and Yvonne guarded the "chemo schedule" with as much seriousness as an executive team making multimillion-dollar decisions. They decided who was allowed to sit in those chairs while I was in the infusion suite and how long they could stay. It was quite an operation. So many people wanted to get on that list—people from work, people from church, and even people who wanted to fly in from other parts of the country. I thought it was beautiful, and if it had been up to me, they all could have come in, but my posse was ruthless about saying no.

Even Lisa's husband, Rick, the one who'd had cancer himself, had trouble getting on the list. He eventually did an end run around the schedulers and went to Kenny, who then came to me. "Rick wants to come and sit with you next week." Of course I wanted that, too. Rick knew more than almost anyone what I was going through. I went to my gatekeepers and said, "You need to stop. This is what I want to happen." But even with me, they'd push back. "Well, he can come for a couple of hours, but I don't know if he can stay the whole time."

❧

The infusion room, to be honest, was pretty bland and usually very quiet. On my first round, I'd noticed that the chemo patients all sat in their chairs without talking to one another. They'd put in their headphones and listen to their music or whatever, or they'd converse with the person there with them, almost in a whisper. Everyone always looked serious.

I knew right away that wasn't going to work for me.

So as I walked into the infusion suite for my fourth session, I stopped to take in the change to the room.

I had come in the Friday before to set up the decorations so that the folks coming in on Monday could also enjoy them. My theme that week was March Madness, not just because I love sports, and wanted to show off my Berkeley blue and gold, but also because cancer was putting us all though our own "March madness."

I'd talked to all of the staff and patients in advance and found out their favorite basketball teams and what colleges, if any, everyone went to. I'd brought in specific jerseys and banners for each person, and I personalized and decorated all of the chemo stations. There were balloons everywhere shaped like basketballs. The caterer I hired that week provided classic "game food"—hot dogs and buffalo wings and chips. It was all the treats they told us that we shouldn't be eating, but if there was ever a reason for a break in the health food rules, I figured chemo was it.

We talked basketball that day and did a few quizzes to test our sports knowledge. People were sharing stories from their college, or from when their children and grandchildren played sports. Those of us who were cheerleaders laughed, remembering our old routines. The nurses grooved around the playlist of sports-themed songs, while the chemo patients tapped their toes from the comfort of the chemo chairs. It put everyone in a good mood.

Chemo Day had become Party Day.

I've seen plenty of darkness, plenty of life and death, and I can get serious when the situation calls for it. I knew chemo was serious business. It was lifesaving business. But I was convinced it didn't have to be *somber* business. It didn't have to be a place for darkness.

So once a month, we went all out. It got to the point where, any time I showed up, my fellow chemo patients started asking if today was a party day. If not, could we *make* it a party day? They were catching on to what my family has known for years: I'm always ready for the party. I'm ready to laugh, and more important, whether I'm at home, at work, at church, or with friends, I'm ready to make others laugh.

(When I was growing up, my mother wouldn't even sit next to me in church, because she says I was always cracking jokes under my breath. I couldn't help it. The associate pastor really looked a lot like the bear on the front of the Sugar Crisp cereal box, and every time he stood up to preach, I was moved by the Spirit to hum the TV commercial theme song.)

Sometimes, even on the non-party chemo days, I'd put away my briefcase and headphones after a couple of hours and start taking food orders. The nurses would put their brought-from-home lunches back in the fridge, and we would eat and laugh any darkness right out of that room.

What can I say, I like to have a good time. When people ask Kenny, "Is she always like this?" (and that happens a fair amount), he just rolls his eyes and assures them that I'm not faking it. I like to be *alive*. At chemo I might not have been alive *and well*, but I was still breathing, and that was something to celebrate every day. In the darkest moments, I was still looking for the light.

"We've got to remember we're alive," I told someone who asked why I spent my limited "feeling good" hours on something like this. I couldn't promise my fellow chemo patients that they would beat the cancer, but I could help them remember not just to breathe but to live. To seize every day we had. No one, I told them, should ever walk past this room and wonder if we still had breath in our bodies.

14

Letting Go

From the beginning of my fifth pregnancy, I was on total bed rest; I wasn't even allowed to walk to the bathroom. I also had an IV that kept me nourished and hydrated despite the nausea. Fifteen years before I met Winston, I named my IV, as well as the bucket by my bed where I could throw up.

Yes, it was a lot to go through for a baby. Kenny would walk by the room and just shake his head. But when I made it past the sixteen-and-a-half-week mark, I was sure I'd finally figured it out. I was going full term. This was going to be our baby.

We did something we'd never had the chance to do in our other pregnancies. We decorated a nursery. We allowed ourselves to see a future with our baby.

Then, at twenty and a half weeks, *bam,* the labor started.

It was as if the Lord wanted to remind me that there were no guarantees.

My doctor hospitalized me and stopped the labor by putting

me into a bed so inverted that I was almost upside down, to keep the pressure off my uterus. Then he prescribed heavy-duty magnesium to prevent contractions. If I could stay like that for three weeks, he said, I would have a shot at giving birth to a two- or three-pound baby with a chance to survive.

I wanted this baby so much that I was sure I would try anything, but after a week of upside-down life I told Kenny I couldn't do it anymore. The magnesium made me hallucinate, I couldn't recognize anyone, and being upside down made me sick.

"This isn't natural," I told him. "We have to unplug everything." I wasn't sure what the Lord's plan was for my child, but I knew this wasn't it, and I was finally ready to listen.

At twenty-one and a half weeks pregnant, I went into hard labor and gave birth to our first girl. We named her Karolyn, after my mother, Carolyn, but with Kenny's initial, because from the time that little one-pound two-ounce baby was born, she looked just like her daddy.

We called her Special K.

The medical team rushed her to Oakland's neonatal intensive care unit (NICU), where doctors told us she would probably live for only a day or two. Spend as many minutes with her as you can, they told us.

Special K lived through those two days, and then through the first week, and then through the first month. Five separate times, the NICU staff told us to prepare to lose her because one organ or another was shutting down, and five times that tough little girl pulled through surgery. She was a fighter.

I basically lived in the NICU for the first four months. Kenny went back to work, but I stayed near Special K's bed. I probably drove the nurses crazy. I know I drove myself crazy, with more mental energy than could be contained in such a dark, somber place.

The only way for someone like me to get through a day in the NICU was to get in everyone else's business, so I made the rounds every day. I sang to the babies. I got to know the staff and helped them make their shift schedules. I talked to the other parents, encouraging and praying with them whenever I could. The NICU is a place of life-and-death decisions almost every day, and I spent long hours with mothers and fathers who agonized over whether it was time to say goodbye to an infant. I'd counsel them, "This is your baby, and you know when it's time."

And I'd talk to Special K, and I'd ask her about her timing as well. My baby girl kept living, and kept surprising the doctors and everyone around her, day after day. But she was on twenty different meds at one point, and she looked like more tubes than baby. How much more was she going to have to go through? By then I was ready to listen to the Lord and to keep my plans on hold. "Honey, if you're ready to stop fighting, if you need to give up, you just go. I know you're tired. There's a place much better than this, with no tubes and no needles. If you need to go there, we'll be just fine."

In between my visits, I tried to learn as much as I could about the different challenges Special K faced, especially chylothorax, a condition where fluid was steadily building up around her undeveloped lungs.

One afternoon, while I sat by Special K's bed and read a medical journal article about chylothorax, I noticed a footnote that described a new procedure to treat infants with the condition. With nothing to lose that I wasn't already on the verge of losing, I called the researcher listed on the article, who happened to be in Kenny's hometown of Fresno.

I explained who I was, and who Special K was, and some of her problems. The doctor sounded hopeful at first. He described the procedure developed by some of his colleagues in Virginia, which put tiny shunts around an infant's lungs to drain away fluid that the body couldn't handle. It had been 100 percent successful, he said.

"How old is your daughter?" he asked. I told him four months.

There was a silence, almost a sigh, on the other end of the phone. The surgery worked, he said, but it needed to be done in the first two months of a baby's life, before the trauma started stressing or shutting down other systems.

Well, I decided, my baby was strong. Maybe she could have the surgery anyway. I took my findings to Special K's surgical staff at Children's Hospital Oakland. They pushed back a little at first. It was hard for them to accept that there was something they not only hadn't tried but didn't even know about, especially since it was right there in a medical journal I'd borrowed from them! Eventually, though, I persuaded them to talk to the Fresno and Virginia doctors, and everyone got excited about the possibilities.

Karolyn was the first child in Oakland to have the new chylothorax surgery, and she improved so much in the weeks afterward that her doctors started talking about sending her home. She responded well to all their tests, and while she still needed a respirator to breathe for her, most of the other tubes and medicines were removed. She'd gained weight and passed the four-pound mark.

I started to believe that we'd turned the corner.

I was back at work by that point—something the hospital and I agreed was best for all of us—but stopped at the NICU every day to see her. One Thursday night, just before her seven-month birthday and about a week before Special K was scheduled for discharge, something about my daughter didn't feel right. Special K wasn't moving around the way she usually did. She didn't grab my finger when I touched her hand.

The nurse on duty blew off my concerns. The monitors all said Special K was fine.

I went home but couldn't sleep that night. In the darkness, I thought about what I had told so many parents in the previous months, about knowing when to let go. I prayed. *Lord, let these people see what's going on with my baby. If she's coming home this week, great. But if she's ready to go home with you, that's okay, too.*

At four o'clock the next morning, I still couldn't sleep, so I called the NICU. "She's fine, Cynt," the night nurse told me. "She's stronger every day."

I had to take their word for it. I drove across the bridge to my office in San Francisco and checked in halfheartedly on a weekly conference call, but I couldn't pay attention to what was happening. The nurse had said Special K was okay, but something still wasn't right in my soul. I hung up the conference call mid-conversation and called the NICU again. This time, Karolyn's favorite nurse, Janie, was there. I told her about my previous call and my uneasiness.

Janie didn't blow me off. "I just checked on her," she said. "I'm worried, too. She's not moving."

I raced back across the bridge to Oakland, and as soon as I got to the hospital and saw my daughter, I knew she was gone. The respirator still blew air into her lungs, but my baby's soul wasn't there anymore.

The doctors weren't convinced. By that point, everyone in the NICU knew Special K. They loved her. They didn't want to think about losing her. When I asked for an EEG to show whether she still had brain waves, they stalled.

"Don't give up now, Cynt," they said. "You're always the optimist."

I was still an optimist, I said, because I knew my baby was in heaven, without pain, at that very minute. From the time she was born, I'd told Karolyn that if she got too tired and needed to leave, that would be all right. We would miss her, but it would be okay. Now that moment had come, but no one believed me.

For a day and a half, we were at an impasse. The doctors said Special K was fine. My spirit told me she wasn't. Kenny wasn't sure what to think. He wanted that little girl to live so much.

Finally, after much persistence on my part, on Saturday night they agreed to order an EEG and to meet us on Sunday morning to go over the results. Kenny and I spent the night in the hospital's family quarters rather than driving all the way home, and before I went to sleep, I prayed again. *Lord, let these doctors see what's going on. If she's gone, I need you to give them irrefutable evidence, because they're not ready to let go.*

I slept better that night than I had since Special K was born . . . possibly better than I had since Special K was conceived. I slept so well, in fact, that Kenny and I slept right through our seven o'clock meeting time.

When we finally went stumbling and hurrying down the hall toward the NICU, an hour late, we found a group of doctors and nurses coming out of the door and toward us.

"You can't go in there," blurted one of the nurses. I registered that she was crying before I heard her next words. "Karolyn had a brain bleed."

I stopped walking. I took a breath. So here it was. A brain bleed was a possibility for any premature baby whose blood vessels are so tiny and fragile that any little thing can break them and send blood flowing straight to the brain. It's almost always fatal.

"She has no more brain activity. We're sorry," Special K's doctor told us.

I could feel the pain bubbling up from deep in my soul, but in that moment it still felt far away. Larger in my mind in that moment was the desire to say, "I told you so."

I took another breath. The pain was closer, but the wave had not yet broken. I insisted on seeing my baby. Reluctantly, the staff let me go to her crib, where I found her still hooked up to her respirator, her tiny chest moving up and down. Her head, though, was swollen to twice its normal size.

I'd asked the Lord to give the doctors irrefutable evidence that she was gone, and he delivered.

∽

As we were leaving the NICU, a nurse I'd gotten to know well approached me. "Cynt, can you stay for a minute and talk to the other parents? Karolyn was here for a long time, and they're having a hard time with this."

Kenny's head shot up, and I could see what he was thinking.

His grief turned to protective, righteous anger. Was she really asking me this? That was *our* baby lying back in that room. This was *our* loss. Those other parents had babies still breathing.

The nurse had a point. I'd been in this hospital for months. I knew these parents in ways that he didn't. I knew the staff. I knew how much they were all invested in Special K's story, and we were invested in theirs. They were grieving with us. And on top of that, while we were leaving, and facing a new kind of trauma, they were still in that dark and somber room, with infants who continued to walk the line between life and death. Losing Karolyn just a week before she was going home was a blow to every parent there who hoped to bring their own child home someday.

I asked my sister to go with Kenny to the car and said that I would be there in a few minutes.

I went back to the ward, stopped to kiss Special K one last time, and then walked around the room, hugging and talking with the devastated parents and staff. I don't remember exactly what I said—the wave of grief was still rising—but I know I told them the truth that I held on to. Special K had been with us for a reason, and her life and death were part of the bigger plan. I prayed over all of the other babies in that room, not knowing which, if any, of them would join my daughter soon.

Then I walked to the car, where Kenny and my sister were waiting, and I fell into his arms. We just held each other. I took a deep breath. I wiped his tears. His lips were quivering. Kenny strapped me into the seatbelt with shaking hands. He steadied himself enough to grip the wheel, and we drove away from the NICU for the last time.

❧

Even in death, my baby continued to make her mark on the world.

We arranged for a funeral later that week with a beautiful white oak casket, music, and all of the churchwomen in their white dresses. Wanting to make sure everything was just right, I warned the funeral director that he might need to do some extra work to release the fluids from Special K's brain bleed.

"No, your baby is perfect," he said. "She's so beautiful I couldn't even zip her up in a body bag."

That wasn't what I expected to hear. But when I went to see her, the director was right. Special K's head was the size it had always been, and her skin glowed like a porcelain doll. Once the doctors saw what they needed to see, the swelling had disappeared.

Dozens of people from the NICU came to the funeral, where Special K's doctor gave a eulogy. "Karolyn Marshall was here to teach us that we're not God," he said. He told the assembled crowd—and there was a *crowd* of people to send my baby off that day—about all of the times they thought Special K wasn't going to make it, and how she pulled through every time. He told them about the week they were sure she was getting better, but she wasn't. And he told them about the surgery for chylothorax. "In Oakland, from now on we'll call that the Special K surgery," he said.

∽

After the funeral, Kenny and I went out to the hearse to ride to the cemetery. I had felt calm throughout the day, greeting everyone and thanking them for coming.

When I saw the pallbearers getting ready to put my baby's tiny casket in the back of that car, though, everything stopped. "No, give it to me," I told them. "I carried this baby into the world, and I'm going to carry her back out." I took the casket from them and got into the car, holding my daughter on my lap.

The funeral director looked at Kenny, who backed away and nodded. "Let her do what she needs to do." Then he looked at me.

"This okay?" I asked.

He studied me for a long second. "I watched you bring five

babies into this world, and this is the first time you can carry one back out," he said. "It's okay. Just don't open the casket."

When the funeral guests came out of the church, a few stopped by the hearse to offer condolences or tell us they would go to the grave site with us. I can't imagine what they all thought as they leaned into the car window, only to see me sitting there with a baby-sized casket.

When our pastor went back to his car, his wife, Doris, asked how I was doing.

"She's fine," he told her. "She's so strong that she's holding the casket on her lap."

Doris, who was a good friend, stopped him. "Cynt's sitting in the car with the casket on her lap?" He nodded. "She's not fine," Doris told him. "That's not normal. That's someone in a whole lot of pain."

Trust a woman to be able to see these things. I was not fine that day. In fact, I had not been fine for a long time. But I'd kept moving, staying ahead of the rising tide of grief. I'd spent the week making arrangements for her service, pushing back the darkness by keeping busy. For six months before that, I'd been caught up in the NICU. Now all of that was over, and when Kenny and I came home, I was left with a quiet house and a Minnie Mouse–themed nursery right at the top of the steps. You had to pass it to get to our bedroom.

Kenny took one look up those steps and told me that he wanted to go to Fresno to stay with his parents for the weekend. He said he needed to get away from what happened. I knew what he meant was he needed to be away from that nursery. I told him I understood, and that he should go, but I was going to stay home. I was tired and just wanted to rest.

As he walked out the door that evening, I headed up the steps to go to our bedroom to lie down. I got halfway there before everything inside me crumbled—not just Special K's death, but her time in the hospital, and the four miscarriages before her, and all of the physical and emotional pain of the past ten years. I sank onto that staircase and I wept for hours. I slept at some point and then woke up to cry some more. I released years of built-up emotions on those stairs.

I was still lying there on Sunday afternoon when Kenny came home from Fresno. He looked at me there, in the same clothes I'd been wearing when he left, and shook his head. He didn't say anything, though. We'd been through so much together already that he knew better. It would be many more years before I could talk about what happened.

Instead, he loved me in the best way he could. He got me up, got me showered, and put me to bed.

15

Adjust the Pain Points
(Round 5)

Tuesday, March 15, 2011, 4:25 PM

Hello, my friends, all of our prayers from Round 4 were answered and Round 5 is underway in the Chemo Clubhouse. I was looking forward to my arrival this morning and excited to see what happened with the St. Patrick's Day decorations that I dropped off last week. Well, the clubhouse is beautiful, green and lively and everyone seems to be enjoying the party atmosphere. It feels good to be Blirish this week (Black Irish) and to bring cheer to this winning team. The green goodies that I brought in this morning were not on the list of "anti-cancer" foods. Oh well, we already have or had cancer, so eating sweets and junk food for "one" snack won't hurt us. (I was looking for some green Hostess Ding Dongs but couldn't find any.)

During the last chemo round my doctor held back on

one of my three chemo meds, Oxaliplatin. This drug is designed to treat colon cancer that has spread. It has several side effects and I've experienced most of them—I guess too many—with the most severe being nausea and vomiting, low platelets, decreased white blood cell count, and neuropathy (numbness, cramping and tingling of the hands and feet and the inability to swallow, all triggered by the cold). So, you can well imagine how much better this sister felt last week in the absence of some of these side effects. My doctor felt I needed a little break and he wants to get my platelet count back to normal. I don't know when the Oxaliplatin will return, as it can only be left out of just a few rounds. But whatever it takes to get the job done is fine with me. Only seven more rounds to go after today!

I did continue to experience other chemo side effects and severe bone pain last week, but I am grateful that there is a shot to boost my white blood cell count. I can live with the consequences. When I experience the pain I just tell myself that the shot is working and then I cover up in one of my prayer blankets and let the Lord do His thing. Many thanks to so many of you who have sent me a prayer blanket that you personally prayed over just for MY healing. The blankets are powerful. They keep me reminded of the comforting words of Luke 5:17, "And the power of the Lord was present to heal them." Every time I have wrapped up in one of the prayer blankets, the pain has subsided. My God is a healer!

One night when I was trying to manage the pain and deal with some weird pounding sensation in my head, the Lord let me know how I can assist Him in taking care of me. So here's the new "DNA Plan" that I'm going to be paying more attention to: Devotion, spending more time in conversations and fellowship with God; Nutrition, eating healthier "anti-cancer" foods; and Activity, increasing my daily physical exercise activity.

Friends, I can't tell you how much mango, blueberries, cabbage and other fruits and vegetables I've eaten lately. I know those who really know me don't believe it. But, darlings, when you hear the words "You have colon cancer and it's in your lymph nodes" you will do some strange things. And, when you're told that there's a 75 percent chance that you won't be here 5 years from now without chemotherapy, you will make even more changes in your life.

I am making very good progress. Last week I was able to do much more AT&T work and help the kids with some of their school projects. My energy level is still very low but I continue to gain strength from YOU. My girlfriends in Nashville are wearing pearls every Tuesday in honor of my chemo treatments. My Cary and Dallas friends gave me some chemo pearls that I wear religiously to the clubhouse.

I have a buddy in Dallas who sends me the results of her weekly chats with God. Last week, she said, He told her to tell me "Don't worry about tomorrow." He was reminding me that worry is like a rocking chair—it gives you something to do, but it doesn't get you anywhere!

One of my pals in Washington, DC, sent a box of unfrosted cupcakes accompanied by tubes of frosting. You should have seen the college freshmen frosting and decorating cupcakes as they started Spring break last week. Truly, they were just trying to make me happy, but all of us actually had a lot of fun.

All of you have encouraged me in so many different ways and prayed for me, which means everything! By the way, let's all keep the people and nation of Japan in our prayers, too.

Let me close with some awesome news: two of my sisters had colonoscopies recently and received great reports. So, let me encourage all of you to take care of yourselves. My doctors suspect that I had cancer for a couple of years and didn't know it, even though I had routine annual physicals and other doctor visits. Yes, I know life is busy; that's true for all of us. But PLEASE slow down and handle your medical business. I plan on being around another 51 years (this is my mid-life crisis) and I want all of you to be here to enjoy life with me! I love you and appreciate your faithfulness in walking this journey with me and my family. We are indeed beating cancer! God bless you.

Cynt

By the end of the fourth round of chemo, I was calling one particular drug in the chemo cocktail, Oxaliplatin, "the Mean O."

The Mean O is what sucked away my energy and left me lying on the couch at the end of a chemo round, not even able to crawl up the stairs to my bedroom. The Mean O made utensils slip out of my numb fingers. And most of all, the Mean O didn't let me eat.

Friends, you don't know how important eating is until you can't do it.

When Dr. Eisenbeis said he wanted to leave that particular drug out of my next couple of treatments, I tried to talk him out of it, thinking that anything that was this hard on me must be hard on the cancer cells, too. The sicker I was, the more I must be fighting, right? But my kind and patient doctor explained something my research hadn't brought up: The Mean O wasn't required in every chemo round. Skipping it a couple of times would help me get my strength back, which was also a form of fighting cancer. Plus, instead of nine bad days, he thought I would have only one or two.

I suddenly saw a world where chemo didn't sometimes feel worse than cancer. Right away, I pulled out my calendar. I had some work events in the next few weeks, and Anthony's spring break was coming up. I started telling my oncologist which weeks would be best for me to skip the Mean O and have some extra time and energy.

Dr. Eisenbeis laughed. That's not how this worked, he said. *He* got to decide when to change the cocktail, not me, and it would be based on what my body needed, not what AT&T needed or my kids' sports schedules.

Well, fine.

∞

After Dr. Eisenbeis cut the Mean O in round 4, I went home feeling more energetic than I had in weeks. Mind you, I was still weak, and my bones still ached from those white blood cell shots. Still, I was close enough to feeling like myself that I decided to drive to work and tackle the pile of things that I knew must be on my desk. I hadn't been there in weeks.

I spent the whole drive in to the office thinking about how excited everyone would be to see me. How much they must have missed me. I rode up the elevator imagining the squeals of excitement and the long lists of questions that only I could answer.

When I walked into my office, though, I found that Sylvia—my friend from Georgia who was covering my meetings while I was out—was already there. In fact, she was sitting in *my* office chair, her purse was on *my* table, and worst of all, she was clearly in a meeting and giving instructions to Venessa, *my* chief of staff.

And neither of them squealed. In fact, those women didn't look all that excited to see me.

My voice sounded strained as I greeted them, but I kept my head up as I announced that I would be in my conference room and made a quick retreat. I would wait there in relative privacy, I decided, until they came to greet me and let me know that they'd cleared out of my space. I thought maybe they'd even apologize.

That didn't happen. Instead, my cellphone rang, and I saw it was my boss in Washington, D.C. David wasn't calling to check on my health or to go over my projects for the week, either. No, he was calling because the occupants of my office next door had called him instead of talking to me directly. He reprimanded me for being at the office.

"Go home," he told me, plain and simple.

I tried to remind him that we'd agreed I would still work several hours a week and go to select events. I told him about the Mean O, and that Dr. Eisenbeis said I could come in to the office that week if I felt up to it. None of it mattered. "Go home," he said again. Sylvia was in charge of the office, and my presence was going to confuse things.

I cried in the elevator on the way back to my car. Clearly, my boss either didn't understand or didn't care that he was killing my spirit while I was trying to keep cancer from killing my body.

Yes, okay, that was a dramatic reaction. Did I really expect they would just leave my office empty like a shrine for three months? Well, okay, maybe I did, a little. But I promised to tell you the good, the great, the bad, and the ugly parts of my story, and on that day I wasn't feeling great.

❧

It wasn't long after my failed trip to the office that I got an email that put some things into perspective. JTS, whose real name is John, is a brilliant and caring colleague and friend who lived in another state but had been following my cancer journey online. He took time out of his busy schedule to empathize with my situation. He mentioned that he suspected the hardest part, and the source of much of my frustration, wasn't really the exhaustion, pain, or neuropathy. The hardest part for someone like me—*someone like us,* he actually said—must be living with a sharp mind that goes a hundred miles an hour and a frail body that just couldn't keep up.

Bingo! JTS knew that I needed some reassurance that I still had it going on mentally, even if my body didn't always cooperate. He also knew that what I really needed was a reminder to not try to keep up with my old physical pace. I was desperate to push myself, to prove to everyone, me included, that cancer wasn't going to take me out. I had a life to live, and I wanted to live all of it. But with each round of chemo, as I got progressively sicker and weaker, that determination to push through was taking more of a toll. Even without the Mean O, I still wasn't really ready for everything I wanted to do.

Sylvia and Venessa had seen something I couldn't see that day in my office, and now JTS was giving it words.

It was okay for me to rest my mind for a few weeks to give my body time to catch up. It didn't mean I was giving up.

I needed to learn to think differently about how I approached my life.

When the nausea rolled through my system, instead of resenting it, I used it as a reminder of how good homemade navy bean soup could be, especially the kind made by Lisa's husband, Rick, the one who'd had so much trouble getting in to sit with me in chemo. He'd been through cancer himself when he was just twenty-seven years old, and navy bean soup was the only thing that he could keep down on the really hard days. When he found out I was sick, the first thing he said to his wife was, "I need to make Cynt some soup." He did, and there were plenty of days when that was all I could keep down, too.

When the neuropathy left my fingers and toes ice cold and buzzing with nerve pain, I'd sink into the warm, blissful comfort of a pair of fuzzy socks and gloves. As my kids like to remind me, it wasn't a fashionable look, but ten years later I still have a drawerful of fuzzy socks in all different colors, ready to match my outfit or to share with someone else who needs them.

It was harder to adjust my attitude when my doctor told me that my weakened immune system left me vulnerable to every virus and cold going around, and so I needed sterile masks and gloves whenever I was with other people. Our house was basically Grand Central station, with people from work, from church, and from the neighborhood coming and going all day. It was Southern hospitality at its best, and I loved it. But wearing a mask day in and day out was just too much for me. I decided I was doing more than my share of work to beat this cancer. I had Winston, and white blood cell shots, and chemo brain. This mask thing, I decided, needed to be someone else's project. So with the help of a couple of nurse friends who had access to medical supplies (this was years before COVID-19 put cute face masks in every store), I created a colorful display of sterile masks and surgical gloves in my front hallway and announced that if anyone came over, they needed to don the gear. They could pick a set to match their outfit.

There were days I was stuck in bed, barely able to open my eyes, but I'd see the whole posse there, in their coordinated gloves and masks, and the ridiculousness of it just brightened my day.

None of this is to say I stopped working completely, or never went to my office again. I continued to talk to my team and our stakeholders. But I also started to give myself, and the people around me, more grace to adjust to the changes we all faced.

Thank the Lord for people like JTS who are willing to step up, speak up, and help us see things in a different way.

16

Stay Open

Once I got up off those stairs, I decided that I needed to move on with my life, and the only way I knew how to get ahead of the grief and depression was to throw myself into my work. I've never been a nine-to-five clock-watcher, but after we lost our baby, I was working all day, seven days a week.

I couldn't sleep. Sometimes I couldn't breathe. I knew I was in a bad space, but I couldn't let myself slow down. If I paused, those waves of emotions would rise back up again, and sometimes I thought they might drown me. Kenny saw it, too, but he also knew that confronting me directly wasn't going to change anything. I was gonna do what I was gonna do.

Instead, he turned his own grief toward a new project: planting the seeds for a different kind of family.

Kenny had been talking about the possibility of adoption for years, but I never gave him much attention. In fact, probably the stupidest thing I ever said in my life was to a well-meaning colleague who asked, after one of my miscarriages, if we would consider adoption. "There is no way you can love a kid that somebody else had like you would love your own. It's *impossible*. It's *hooey*," I told him. I cringe as I share those words now, because I was 100 percent wrong. But here we are, with the good, the great, the bad, and the ugly.

Now that it was crystal clear that I wasn't going to have another baby, Kenny started angling in and bringing up adoption again. He'd done his research and knew that the adoption process took a year or two, so it didn't seem as if we were rushing into anything. In the meantime, the meetings and paperwork might get my mind off work and away from our loss. Maybe adoption would help me break out of this depression and focus on the future.

I came home from work one night a couple of months after Special K passed to find him standing at the door, car keys already in hand. There was a meeting we needed to go to that night with the county social workers about adopting locally, he said.

I told him I wasn't going, because it was too soon. In theory, I was all right with adoption. I wanted us to have a family. I wanted to be a mother. But after all of those months in the hospital, I wasn't ready for the bureaucracy and the roller-coaster ride of trying to find a child. I wasn't ready to risk this part of my life not going according to my plan again. I couldn't commit myself to another child when there were so many ways for an adoption to fall through.

If Kenny wanted to adopt a baby right then, I said, that was fine, as long as I didn't have to do anything about it. I told him he needed to just get someone to leave a baby on our doorstep.

One of the things I love about my husband is that with me, he knows when to back off. Sometimes that's not the case with others. He also knows when I need him to step forward. That night, when I was still not in my right mind, Kenny stepped forward, literally. He picked me up and put me in the car. "We're going."

I knew he was grieving, too. I had turned all of my attention back to work, where I was in control, but I could see that he still had a hole of loss that he was looking to fill. For his sake, I grudgingly agreed to go to the meeting. But I went with an attitude, and I made sure that everyone in the room knew that I didn't want to be there.

The social workers weren't looking at me, though. I found out later that as soon as we came in, they looked at Kenny and said to one another, "That man could be Anthony's father."

❦

When my son Anthony was nine months old, his biological mother left him with his nine-year-old brother, Rickey, in the room of an abandoned and crumbling hotel, and she never came back. She got arrested that day—she had a long history of trouble with drugs—and somehow never mentioned to the police that she'd left two kids in an empty building.

Rickey was used to his mom disappearing by that point, and he settled in to once again take care of his baby brother. They mostly stayed in the room, which he heated with an old toaster oven, but when they needed food, Rickey put Anthony in a shopping cart, covered it with a blanket so that no one would see the baby, and pushed it through the neighborhood, looking for anything to scrounge or steal. This went on for two months—two months!—before a couple of unhoused neighbors realized their mother wasn't coming back and told the cops about the unattended kids.

When the police finally got to them, baby Anthony was malnourished, gray, and close to death. But he was alive, and that's only because of his brother.

The state split up the brothers. Anthony went to the hospital and then to a short-term foster family while social workers tried to find an adoptive family for him. That round-cheeked baby passed through at least four foster homes in the following year and a half. In each one, he was neglected, abused, or both. No one ever stepped forward to adopt him. The older he got, the less likely he was to find a home. The hard truth is that there aren't many people looking to adopt two-year-old Black boys. According to the social workers I met that night, most prospective adoptive parents come looking for infant girls.

Finally, the social workers signed paperwork to move Anthony into a long-term group home. It wasn't the same as giving this boy a family of his own, but at least it would give him a stable place to live for the next sixteen years.

Just two hours later, I was sitting in an overheated classroom at our county's administrative building filling out a questionnaire about what I was looking for in an adoption. Well, I wasn't looking for anything yet, but when I got to the question about what kind of child we wanted to adopt, without giving it much thought, I wrote, "Two-year-old Black boy." We'd just lost an infant daughter. I wasn't trying to replace her.

There was a noise behind me. One of the social workers had been reading over my shoulder, and there were tears in her eyes when she grabbed the paper. "Are you sure about this?" she asked, pointing to my answer. Then she told us about Anthony, and then there were tears in our eyes.

I'd told Kenny I wanted a baby if I didn't have to go through all of that process. Now here was a boy, ready and waiting, and all we had to do was say yes.

We said yes.

The next morning, the social worker went to the courthouse, where Anthony's placement papers were already on a judge's desk waiting for a signature, and pulled them off.

Special K died on August 21, 1994. Four months later, the week before Christmas, Anthony came home with us. His placement happened unusually quickly in order to make the transition for him as smooth as possible. I hardly had time to think about it, or to wonder about the timing. Did God delay calling Special K to heaven in order to get us ready for a quick placement with a little boy who already needed us? Was His plan being executed faster than anything I could have dreamed?

What was clear was that my plan was never *the* plan. The Lord knew how our family was being made that year, and it was a story more beautiful than anything I could imagine.

∽

Ten years after our journey to start a family began, we were parents virtually overnight. Our family was finally launched outside a hospital, and Kenny and I had a lot to learn—not just about the normal issues of caring for a toddler, but also the unique challenges of pouring love into a child scarred by neglect, abuse, and abandonment.

I had so many questions about being a mother. Thank God that He had answers.

About a year after we brought Anthony home, he started telling me not to turn out his light after I read him his stories and put him to bed. "Leave it on, Mama, or else they're gonna come and get me."

I would sit on his bed and sing to him and reassure him that no monsters were coming after him. But he would cry until I agreed to leave his light on. He fought sleep and was clearly terrified, and nothing I said seemed to help.

After three or four nights like this, the poor little boy had bags under his eyes. Kenny happened to be in the hallway as I was coming out, again, from a brightly lit room. "Why's the light on?" he asked.

I told him what Anthony said, and added, "You've got to stop watching scary movies and TV shows and stuff with him before I get home. Now he's afraid of monsters."

Kenny shrugged off my scolding and said he would check to see if Anthony was asleep. He went in, and I noticed he stayed in there for a long time. I eventually tiptoed over to the door. Kenny was on the bed, deep in conversation with our son, and he waved me away. A few minutes later, I saw him go downstairs and bring a photo album back to the room.

Finally I heard them laughing, and then it was quiet again.

Kenny came out, turning off Anthony's light on his way out the door.

When we were out of Anthony's earshot, he asked, "What's that boy been telling you all week?"

"I told you. The monsters are coming to get him."

Kenny looked at me. "Did he say 'monsters'?"

I thought. Now that he mentioned it, Anthony only ever said "they" were coming. I'd assumed the part about the monsters.

"No," I admitted. "Who does he think is coming to get him?"

"The people in the white cars."

When Kenny asked his son more specific questions, Anthony said his fears were not about scary creatures in a closet but "the ladies in the white cars." It turned out he still remembered the social workers who had come—in their city-owned white sedans—to take him out of one foster home after another when things went wrong. Anthony told Kenny that the white cars came when people didn't want him anymore, and he'd been with us for so long he was sure it was time for the cars to come again soon. But he didn't want to leave this time, he said. No one beat him here. He got fed. "I don't want to leave you and Mom," he said, crying.

Oh, those scars went deep.

Kenny told me that he cried then, too, and pulled Anthony close as he promised that no one was ever going to take him away. "You belong with us now." That's when he went to get the photo album, full of pictures from the day we brought Anthony home and the day the adoption was official. Kenny showed him the Christmas card we'd sent out that year, with a picture of us all standing with the judge under the caption "He Adopted Us!" He showed Anthony his birth certificate that listed us as his parents. "No one ever gets to take you away from us," Kenny promised. "Not ever. There are no more white cars."

It took a few more minutes to convince him, but finally Anthony got it. He grabbed his dad—his forever dad—and hugged him hard and then told him to turn off the light so that he could finally get some sleep.

17

Celebrate Halftime
(Round 6)

Tuesday, March 29, 2011

Happy Spring from the Chemo Clubhouse! Round 6 began today, which means I am halfway home to a disease free, no chemotherapy, DNA (Devotion, Nutrition, Activity) life-style. Two months ago, someone on my work team told me to draw a big smiley face on March 29th. He said that day would come quickly and I would then spend the next 3 months (April, May and June) coming down the other side of the chemo mountain. I couldn't see that far ahead in January and I'm kind of bossy—but I can also take orders, so I did as he suggested.

Well, here we are at March 29th and, friends, Walter was right! I can actually say, "Ain't No Mountain High Enough." Because of all of your prayers, and the grace of a GREAT BIG God, half of my chemotherapy treatments are behind me and I'm doing better than most people expected. I've climbed the mountain!

During Round 5, even though I wasn't on the heavy-duty chemo regimen (no Oxaliplatin), I still had lots of bone pain from the white blood cell booster shot, to accompany the fatigue and hair loss. I also became very restless mentally. As some of you know, life is a challenge when your body is at 50 percent capacity, but your mind and heart are running at 150 percent. So, in line with my doctor's instructions, I decided to resume some normal activities. I worked a lot this month and engaged even more in some big work projects—and I felt better! I attended Shirley's soccer game on Saturday, provided some "mommy" support—and felt even better! (Ok, before you fuss at me—I know I really shouldn't have been out in bad weather since I don't have an adequate immune system to fight off a cold. But I went to the car at halftime when the weather turned quite cold.) And three times recently a voice told me to do something nice and fun for my three teenagers, my sister and some close friends who have been incredibly available and supportive. So I wrapped up, put on my furry socks and proceeded to administer the medicine most effective in this type of crisis . . . shopping! As I have not been able to engage in my favorite pastime, it was probably "my" voice that told me to leave the house and return with 9 pairs of shoes. But it was great and I've been walking around the house in sweat pants and pumps! Today, I introduced my chemo pump "Winston" to the real pumps. :-)

Looking ahead, I know Round 6 will be more like the first three rounds as we return to the full regimen of heavy duty chemo meds. I will continue to draw strength from the books, cards, flowers, food and many other things that you are sending to me daily. After one of the regular food deliveries one of my daughters asked "where is all of this food coming from?" I told her "Mom has a lot of friends that love us. They don't want us worried about dinner so they've raised a lot of money and arranged meals for us." She replied, "Wow, that's too much. I better get me some friends that love me." I wish she could see the thousands of people like you across this country that love her and all of us. Your outpouring of love is evidence of John 13:35, "By this everyone will know that you are my disciples, if you love one another." Thank you for loving me and my family.

Thank you also for praying for us, especially my children. Ken Anthony was in the Emergency Room at college most of last night dealing with a torn cartilage in his sternum. I thank the Lord for good friends who insisted on taking him to the hospital. He was in pain all day but still going to class and working on an upcoming production (that's my boy). At midnight, he told me not to drive to the hospital because he needed me to focus on chemo today. I'm trying to obey—again, bossy but can take orders. Please keep him in your prayers.

Throughout this experience, I have been constantly reminded of the promise of 2 Corinthians 12:9, "My grace is sufficient for you for my power is made perfect in weakness." I have had many weak days since Dec. 15, 2010 (my 51st birthday). I've had to battle cancer and some other things simultaneously. I've had days where I just looked up and asked the Lord to give me strength. Inevitably, those were the days when I would receive a card, email or phone call with the message "Rely on His strength. His grace is enough. Let go and Let God." Time and time again YOU knew just what to say and when to say it.

Your visits have also kept me going. Some of you just routinely pop in with goodies (the latest—homemade bread and meatballs). You have no idea how powerful and encouraging your words have been to my spirit. But trust me when I say that God has truly used you to minister to us. Your prayers are getting us through every trial that arises.

Okay, that's it for now. It is March 29th (thank you Walter) and I am starting Round 6 with the right ATTitude. It will be rocking in the clubhouse this week as we wrap up March Madness. No matter how difficult, I'm halfway home and fully aware that His grace is sufficient! I love you,

Cynt

Round 6 was just as hard as I suspected it would be. After a couple of weeks off from the Mean O, going back to a full round of the chemo cocktail was brutal. On top of the nausea and exhaustion, my white blood cell count had stayed dangerously low, which meant I needed those cell-boosting shots again. They were almost as bad as the Mean O.

Round after round, I kept getting weaker, and my lab results kept getting worse. After the debilitating sixth round, Dr. Eisenbeis asked for a meeting to discuss the situation. I was ready for him and had my list of questions all laid out. But my oncologist didn't look at me or talk to me that day as he usually did. Instead, he left me shivering in the chair and focused all of his attention on Kenny, who had shown up with his own concerns about my health.

I sat back for a while and watched them talk about me as if I weren't in the room. I listened to the doctor say that he would put my chemo on hold for a few weeks to give me a chance to rebuild some strength, and I heard Kenny agreeing that would be best. I let them get right up to the point where Dr. Eisenbeis started telling a nurse what my new schedule was.

Then I stepped in.

"Excuse me, did either of you ask me what I thought about this plan?" Both men just looked at me. "I'm sitting right here. *I'm* the one having chemo. *I'm* the one who gets to decide, and *I* say we're going to continue with the next round."

Dr. Eisenbeis—who really is a good guy, even if he forgot that day whom he was dealing with—looked a little startled, and he made the mistake of glancing back at Kenny. My husband knew enough to look away. I could almost see him thinking, *Here we go with her plans again.*

My final round of chemo was scheduled for June 23. I had it all mapped out. I knew I would still need a couple of days with Winston after that and then would go back a month later for a final round of tests, but I had no intention of being back in this building ever again after the month of July. Postponing my treatments would prolong this season, and it would mess with my plans. I wasn't having it. I had made it to halftime, and I had no intention of slowing down.

"No, no, don't look at him. Look at me," I told Dr. Eisenbeis. "My husband doesn't have a say here. This is my body, and I know that chemo is what's saving my life, even if you two seem to have forgotten. I've got this. We'll continue."

Kenny just rolled his eyes.

∽

The truth is, my cancer was hard on my husband. He really struggled watching me suffer, especially after all of the things we'd already been through. Kenny felt as if he'd already done his time watching me suffer miscarriage after miscarriage, and the endless rounds of medical offices and procedures were hard on him. He never really got past that first reaction, worrying about what the family would do without me. What he would do without me.

"This ain't right," he told Anthony at one point. "That's my wife. I've known that woman since she was fifteen years old, and I'm not ready for something to happen to her. Not ready for her to be gone." He looked at our son. "If something happened to you, your brother, or your sisters, I'd feel really bad. It would be horrible. But if something happens to your mother . . ." He didn't finish the thought. Anthony said he didn't have to.

Our pastor tried to encourage Kenny to pray about how he was feeling, but Kenny wasn't having that, either. "I'm not feeling it," was all he said. "This ain't cool."

I love that even after decades together Kenny and I are still polar opposites, bringing different strengths to our relationship, and yet at the same time we have always wanted the same things out of life. We both prioritize stability and peace. And we both value faith, albeit in different ways. He appreciates church and the community it brings, but he's less inclined to seek out a personal connection with God for comfort or deliverance.

I truly never got angry about having cancer, but Kenny surely did, and I met plenty of people like him while I was in chemo, especially some of the loved ones and family members of those of us who were sick. It's hard being sick, but I think sometimes it's even harder watching the person you love being sick.

All through my chemo treatments, he was with me every step of the way, but inside, emotionally, he was in a bad place. He's naturally the cynical pessimist to my optimist. I call him my Mr. Negative, because he'll always be the one to point out the worst-case scenario. And sometimes I need to hear that from him. He balances me, just as he balances our family.

Our kids will tell you that if they need to get something done, I'm the best option. Mom always has a plan, and I can be relentless about getting to the best possible outcome as fast as possible. But their dad is the processor in the family. If they want to talk about something for a long time, work their way through their thought process, or unpack the pros and cons of a decision they need to make, they go to Dad.

Family is everything to my husband, and I love that maybe most of all, but it meant that my cancer hit him hard, because to him it threatened what he held most dear. Sure, Shirley was the one who would tell everyone, including me, that I was about to die, but from the first day, I knew Kenny thought it. He was where she was, but he held all of that anger and grief inside.

I prayed so much for my healing, not just because I wanted to live, but because I wanted to show him what God could do. I was halfway done, just holding on and waiting for June 23.

18

Believe in Miracles

The first time I met Dr. Eisenbeis, I asked him if he believed in miracles.

"I think so," he said with a bit of a smile and a bit of an expression that said, "Is this woman crazy?" I ignored the latter part and grabbed his hands while I told him that I hoped he did, because he was about to be part of a miracle.

"Cancer is my midlife crisis," I told him. "I'm going to live to be 102." I said that stage 3 or not, I had already decided I was going to live and that cancer would become the new way for me to encourage others. Together, he and I would show the world that you can beat this and thrive, but I needed to know up front if he was on board. Did he see me as some lost cause, or was he ready for the fight?

He didn't exactly agree with me, but he didn't say no. And for a man of medicine and science, that was saying a lot. Months later, Dr. Eisenbeis admitted he went home after our first meeting and told his wife about the woman who asked him if he believed in miracles, because no patient had ever talked to him with so much certainty about an unknown outcome.

∞

I grew up in a hardcore Pentecostal church, which means that I grew up seeing and hearing about modern miracles. As a child I witnessed pastors laying their hands on people in wheelchairs, who then got up and walked. As an adult, I've personally experienced healing I consider miraculous.

When I was twenty-eight and climbing the corporate ladder, I was under so much stress that I had a bleeding ulcer. It got so bad the doctor said I needed surgery, which I didn't want. I went home and prayed as hard as I knew how. When I went in for the next visit, the ulcer was gone. It took some doing to convince the doctors that I hadn't gone to another medical professional for treatment.

And then there's Kenny's story.

When Anthony was about three years old, he brought home a virus from daycare, the way that kids—basically small germ carriers—tend to do. We all got sick, and the doctors put the whole family on a strong antibiotic. The medicine was sulfur-based, though, and we found out that Kenny's allergic to sulfur. He had a nasty reaction, so his doctor told him to stop taking it.

A day or two later, I came home from work carrying a bag of chili cheese dogs for dinner. (This was obviously in the days before I started trying to eat healthier.) When I came in, I could hear Anthony playing upstairs with my niece Gynelle, who was a teenager at the time and always over at our house. I went downstairs to the TV room to check on Kenny and bring him his requested dinner.

As soon as I saw him lying on the couch, I threw my hands in the air in shock and the hot dogs went flying. My husband's whole face was twisted, and half of it drooped as if he'd had a stroke.

He heard me and turned and tried to say something—probably to ask me what I had done to his hot dogs—which was how Kenny realized he couldn't speak. He'd been alone down there for a couple of hours, napping and watching TV, and hadn't felt what was happening to his face.

I don't know why I didn't just call an ambulance, but in the moment I was convinced I needed to take my husband to the emergency room myself. I shouted upstairs to Gynelle, telling her to keep Anthony with her, while I half lifted, half dragged my two-hundred-pound husband off the couch and up the stairs. I even physically lifted him into the passenger seat of his big truck.

But wait, that's not the miracle.

In the emergency room, a doctor too young to be sure of himself examined Kenny and ran some tests but couldn't find anything definitively wrong. There was no sign of a stroke, despite his symptoms. "If I didn't know better, I'd say it was viral encephalitis," he said. "Something from your son's virus may have broken the blood-brain barrier." But encephalitis is incredibly rare and isn't usually caused by something as common as a bug brought home from daycare. The young doctor confessed he really didn't know what he was looking at. When Kenny started talking again, the hospital sent us home and told us to watch for new symptoms. That didn't seem right, but I went with it.

A couple of days later, I was walking out of the house, on my way to work, when I saw Kenny's truck zigzagging erratically down our street. He'd been feeling a little better and took Anthony to daycare that morning, but on his way back something had clearly gone wrong. When he pulled up to the house, he could barely get out of the car.

I took him to a different emergency room this time, but the doctors there didn't know what was wrong, either. They ran more tests and got more inconclusive results. They tried to send him home again, but this time I wasn't having it. Whatever was happening was still obviously a problem. The doctors and I had some words, and they found out how hard it was to tell me no.

Finally, after a couple of days and no improvement or diagnosis, I tracked down the head of neurology, who did his own examination and came back agreeing with the original emergency room doctor: viral encephalitis. Anthony's daycare bug had gotten into Kenny's brain somehow and was attacking his motor skills.

Most cases of viral encephalitis resolve within a few weeks, but instead of getting better, Kenny got worse. It was awful. My husband lost the ability to walk, then to talk. He couldn't respond to us when we visited. The doctors started warning me that this would likely lead to permanent brain damage.

After weeks in the hospital, we moved Kenny to a rehab hospital in Berkeley. He still couldn't walk or talk. Following the hospital's instructions, I hired contractors to make our house wheelchair accessible, with railings and ramps everywhere.

Things were not looking good for the Marshalls.

The truth is, though, that even when things were bleak, I knew that this was not going to be our story. I knew, deep in my soul, that God did not bring Anthony to our family only to immediately have his new dad become disabled. God did not give me a son to raise alone while also caring for a husband who couldn't walk or talk.

The idea that this was something permanent was too much.

My spirit would not accept it.

Instead, the more I prayed, the more I saw that this was prime space for the Lord to do a miracle.

∽

As the summer progressed and Kenny didn't, I started thinking about an upcoming church convention that my mother and sisters and I attended every year. It was the kind of Spirit-filled gathering where thousands of people, including hundreds of Black prayer warriors in classic white church dresses, gathered every morning for the most intense conversations with the Lord you've ever seen.

It was the kind of event where miracles happen.

I knew I needed to go to that convention in order to get my miracle. I wasn't going for entertainment. I wasn't going for a vacation. I was going there to pray like I'd never prayed before, without distraction and in the company of His saints.

The hospital staff made it clear to me that they didn't like my plan. They even had the staff ethicist lecture me about how irresponsible it was to fly off to South Carolina when my husband was in this condition. I guess they didn't know a lot of people in Berkeley going off to church conventions. But I didn't back down.

I was going for a miracle, and they couldn't talk me out of it.

This was the time to advocate, not just for my family, but also for my faith.

I took Anthony with us, knowing that my mom and sisters would help take care of him, and Kenny's parents agreed to drive up from Fresno to stay in our house and keep an eye on him. Gynelle would help where she could.

Things at home started going sideways as soon as I left. Gynelle called me on the second day to report that Kenny's parents never arrived. His mother, it turned out, decided she couldn't bear to see her only son—in his mid-thirties and the prime of his life—laid out in a bed like that, and so she made her husband turn the car around and take her home. Gynelle, all of seventeen years old, stepped up and went to the rehab hospital to be with Kenny. (Her mother was with me at the convention, but her dad was with her, so she wasn't totally alone.)

That's when I knew for sure that this trip, and this situation, was a way for the Lord to build my faith.

I stayed at the convention, but I called and talked to the hospital staff every afternoon. The report was always the same. *Still no change.*

I prayed. The women in the white dresses prayed.

Friday passed. Saturday passed. Sunday passed. *Still no change.*

Finally, on Monday, when I called the hospital, the nurse who answered the phone said something different and totally unexpected.

"We don't know where he is."

What?

I thought the nurse sounded a little panicked, either at losing a patient or at telling me, I wasn't sure which. "He's not in his room. We'll call you back." And she hung up.

I found out later that Kenny woke up on Monday morning with a single, clear thought: *I should take a walk.* He didn't question why he was in a hospital or why he needed to walk. He just got out of bed and started walking—something he couldn't do the day before. He went out of his room, down the hall, and to the elevator. No one stopped him. No one even noticed.

When he got to the elevator, he saw a wheelchair sitting there, and so he sat in it. I don't know exactly why, since he was already walking. All he tells me now is that he wanted to sit. He rolled himself in his new wheelchair onto the elevator, through the lobby, and then out the front door of the building and into the sun. When the nurses finally found him, hours later, he was sitting there just soaking in the rays.

When he saw them coming, he thought they looked mad, and so he opened his mouth and discovered he could also talk.

"I guess my wife's looking for me?"

They rolled him back inside and to a phone—this was still the 1990s, before the proliferation of cellphones—and called me.

"It's a miracle," the nurse told me before she handed him the phone.

I left Anthony at the convention with my mom and sisters and flew back to California that afternoon. I had my miracle.

Kenny's road to full recovery was slow, but in the months that followed, he regained almost all of his mobility and speech. We hired the contractors again to take down all of the ramps and bars in the house. The doctors say his long-term brain damage is minimal, and he's 85 or 90 percent back to normal.

I jokingly say that's less brain damage than the boy had when I married him.

19

Get Straws, Gloves, and Fuzzy Socks (Round 7)

Wednesday, April 13, 2011

Round 7 is underway in the chemo clubhouse and His grace is sufficient for this day! My lab work looked good this morning, with evidence of slight anemia. The chemotherapy resumed today with powerful Oxaliplatin and the white blood cell booster shot being a part of this round's medicines. Thank goodness for the nasty stuff as it is necessary for my full recovery. It's like when my parents used to give us kids Castor Oil, convincing us that it cured everything—even if it didn't taste good. Fortunately, I have something within me that is better than Castor Oil and far more powerful than the side effects of these chemo meds! My God is greater than any force that is in this world (1 John 4:4).

Your prayers and God's grace will take me through Round 7. I'm really looking forward to the miracles that are in store. Day 1 of this round has been the most difficult Day 1 so far. Many side effects are already present and it looks like I will be wrapped up in all of my prayer blankets over the next few days. By the way, thank you for the blankets and the prayers that went into each one of them.

The "O" medicine (Oxaliplatin, not Oprah) is what a friend of mine calls "the mean medicine." It caused the neuropathy to return in full force during Round 6. The inability to swallow worsened and I found myself getting my nourishment through a straw on some days. All of the usual side effects returned and I was nowhere near normal until the ninth day, but the Lord gave me enough strength to resume some of my normal activities. And I took full advantage, as I always do, of my five "good" days. Instead of shopping for handbags to match my new shoes, I spoke at a "Cuts for Cancer" event at High Point University on April 7, World Health Day. This terrific event was organized and hosted by the Freshman class, many of whom cut and donated their hair for wigs for cancer patients. I am so proud of this generation of young people. They have a heart for service and giving and for doing what God has called us all to do—be our brother's keeper (sistah's too). My son, Ken Anthony, surprised me and made a quick appearance between classes from his nearby university, UNC School of the Arts. Seeing Antman and his two friends was good medicine for me. I just wish I could have figured out how to get these young talented artists to grab some of that hair and fill in my bald spots. Oh well, I guess I will just keep doing the Donald Trump thing for a little while longer. I see a very short haircut in my future to go with the 10 pound weight loss.

As we prepared to begin Round 7, and I thought about the medicines I would be receiving, I claimed one of the most precious Biblical promises: "And we know that all things work together for the good to those who love God, who have been called according to his purpose" (Romans 8:28). Everything that is happening on this journey is for a good reason and we will make good out of it. In fact, we will make "great" out of some of it!

I am so grateful for your continued commitment to this journey. Your words and expressions of love are so comforting and show up at just the right time. Last week at almost midnight I received an email from one of our senior level employees, who I know has very little time to send me an email. He just wanted to check on me and to express how difficult it must be for me to not have my normal energy level. His thoughtfulness and words were quite touching.

Another one of my friends is continuing her chats with God. He told her to tell me to REST, REFRESH and RELISH in His light. She went on to sing on paper, I heard the voice of Jesus say, "come unto me and rest; lay down, thou weary one, lay down thy head upon my breast." This message was so timely as I have not been able to get a good night's sleep. The chemo meds also cause hot flashes and restlessness so I am often in a sleep deprived state. I actually escaped menopause and now chemo brings the hot flashes! Gotta love it. Please pray that I am able to REST during this round. I want to physically rest in my bed all night and spiritually rest in Him. I desire to REFRESH my nutrition commitment by eating healthy and drinking lots of water. And, I want to RELISH in His light and His word during these last 72 days of the journey. I have no doubt that this illness is for a divine purpose and I want to carry out the purpose in a way that glorifies God and gives hope to others.

Well, I was going to tell you about the rest of my family and about some of my work fun and the great day I had with my wonderful team in the office yesterday. However, the neuropathy has affected the nerves in my hands so I can't type anymore right now. Know that I love you very much and I just can't imagine being on this awesome journey without all of you. You are my heroes. You have busy lives that you've decided now include me. I am definitely the most loved person on the planet. THANK YOU! Your love and prayers are making a difference.

    Cynt

I'm convinced that no one, ever, has had a better team of people to pick them up than the people who gathered around me and my family through my chemo treatments. Looking back more than a decade later, what I most remember about that year is the way that when we needed them most, a community of people came together and showered love on me, my family, and one another. I didn't conquer cancer on my own. I did it in the middle of a community.

For years I had poured myself into people, and the year I had cancer, people poured right back into me. Friends and neighbors arranged to get Alicia and Shirley to all their activities so my girls could keep a relatively normal routine. (Kenny, let's face it, would have been happy to let them drop some things so that he didn't have to attend as many dance recitals.) I received package after package from all across the country, full of life-giving gloves and socks. Kids in our neighborhood put colon cancer awareness ribbons on their prom clothes. Colleagues I hadn't seen for years wrote letters and made phone calls.

Two of my dear Tar Heel sisters even organized an outreach to get me personalized, autographed copies of two of my favorite books, *Amazing Peace* by Maya Angelou and *The Power of Nice* by Linda Kaplan Thaler and Robin Koval. (A side story: I met Maya Angelou a few years after this, when she was the presenter of an award I was blessed to receive. She rose from her wheelchair and led the audience in a standing ovation . . . for Kenny. She praised him for giving up his career to take care of our kids and support my career. To this day, he says it's the most touching gesture any-one has ever made toward him.)

And they shared *so much food.*

❧

When my AT&T colleagues first found out that I had cancer, I'm told they had to stop the meeting. Everyone was just in shock. When the employees found out, calls flooded my office, coming not just from North Carolina but also from Georgia, California, Texas, and New Jersey.

As I said earlier, my job had touched a lot of people over the years, and I'm a people person. So when things went wrong, I wasn't just some anonymous name on the staff list. People knew me. I always say that my work colleagues feel like family. Their outpouring of love, concern, and support, at the time when I most needed it, showed me that many of them felt the same way.

After a couple of weeks, the flood of inquiries hadn't let up, and my buddy Patrick, a VP in our Charlotte office, finally orga-nized a giant conference call for anyone who wanted to be part of supporting our family. I wasn't there, but I'm told there were of-fice people, church people, and friends from all over the country, all pushing on one another's nerves with the best of intentions. The call was just wild, with too many ideas and not enough agree-ment, until someone said, "This needs to stop. What would Cynt do if she was here with us?"

"She would start singing Aretha Franklin," someone else said, and that broke the tension. (They were right, by the way. I don't put up with people yelling in my meetings, and if things start get-ting out of control, I'll turn up a reminder for a little "R-E-S-P-E-C-T.")

After the music got the conversation calmed down, everyone had their say and Patrick concluded that the group should orga-nize a system for our family to have meals for as long as we needed it. He said no one in the Marshall house should be distracted by the need to cook.

My executive assistant, Connie, pushed back. "Cynt's in chemo," she said, just full of emotion. "I've seen her. She can't eat anything. She can't keep food down. Why would she want *food*?" Being on the front line with me was hard on Connie, who has a tender heart and hates to see people suffer.

Patrick insisted. "Because Kenny and the kids need to eat," he told her. "And so Cynt's going to be worried about that, and she'll be trying to do too much and feed everybody, and we can take that worry away."

He was right. For the whole length of time I had chemo, I never once had to think about whether my kids needed a meal. Local friends brought home-cooked food a few times a week. One friend left homemade bread on our front step almost every Sunday while we were at church, so we'd have something when we got home. Meanwhile, the national AT&T community funded an account with a local Cary delivery service to provide restaurant food in between, whenever we needed something.

My kids loved it. In fact, I think on some level they were a little disappointed when my chemo ended, because the free food ended with it.

For as long as they can remember, Kenny and I have told our kids about the importance of the village—how in times of need the Lord calls us to come together as a community and take care of one another, and to accomplish what would be impossible alone. They know that I see myself as the product of the village, and the blessings we enjoy happened because of the people who poured into me, into my schools, and into my neighborhood. I wouldn't be where I am today without the teachers, the scholarships, the activism, and all of that. I want my children to be part of this chain of service and community.

But listening to Mom and Dad talk about the importance of giving and sharing is one thing. Seeing it in action is something much bigger. When I got cancer, my kids had a front-row seat to a crisis, and they saw the best examples of how the village can respond to a need. They saw strangers step up and come to our rescue time after time. They saw people give anonymously, not seeking attention.

Having cancer might have been the best gift I ever gave my children, because they understood in a new way not just how God works but how the village works as well.

20

Do You

Nineteen years after my first boss told me to take out my braids before I came back to work, I had moved up the ranks to become one of the youngest vice presidents at Pacific Bell, which had merged with Southwestern Bell. I'd climbed further and faster than I'd ever dreamed.

Then, one night, my boss called me at home.

"I have some good news for you," she said, though her voice didn't sound happy. "The board just met, and they selected you to be an officer of the corporation."

I was shocked. I knew I was doing well, but an *officer*? That was the highest level a person could go, and I was barely forty. It would make me a top shareholder—an owner, in other words—of Southwestern Bell, not just an employee. There were only 110 officers in a company of 200,000 employees, and at the time only two of them were Black women.

This was a *very* big deal for a girl from Easter Hill.

"Congratulations," my boss said, though she didn't sound as if she meant that, either. Truth was, we didn't have a close relationship. Some thought she was not the best fit for her job. She seemed to think I was unsophisticated. But she was my boss, and so I worked hard to support her. And she knew it was me who made her look good.

"Thank you," I said. I could tell Kenny was listening to my end of the conversation. When I said, "Becoming an officer is quite an honor," his eyes got big. He'd worked for Pacific Bell for a time, and so had his dad. He knew what being an officer there meant.

Then my boss shifted gears.

"Of course, you'll need to cut your hair," she said. No, I hadn't gone back to braids or grown out an Afro. I had a totally respectable corporate style, but this woman had the nerve to tell me that she thought I would look better, and "more like an officer," in a shorter cut. Then she gave me the name of a clothing brand that I should buy. She told me to wear more white, because it would complement my skin color. "I left a magazine on your desk," she said. "There are Black people in it, and they're wearing white, and they're just stunning. One of them even has the short haircut I was talking about."

"You want me to cut my hair?" I asked, trying to keep up. What did that have to do with a promotion?

Kenny was still listening. "I have a barber! We'll make you an appointment!" he whispered loudly. He didn't just know what being an officer meant; he knew how much they made. I waved him away, trying to listen to the woman's demands, which were still growing.

"You shouldn't be Cynt anymore. You'll need to be Cynthia. Cindy, maybe, but not Cynt." She sniffed. "No one knows what that is."

"Black people know what that is," I shot back. My attitude was coming out, but she ignored me. Being Cynt in corporate America had often been a challenge. Black women named Cynthia often used the nickname Cynt. But white women, I learned, mostly called themselves Cindy.

I'd been Cynt my whole life. When I was on the track team in high school, everyone called me Cynt the Sprint. But my first few bosses at Pacific Bell regularly called me Cindy, no matter how often I corrected them. I tried to roll with it, but after twenty years, talking about my name was getting old.

And yet my supervisor on the phone, supposedly calling with good news, *still* wasn't done.

"I don't want you to talk so loudly anymore," she said. "Or laugh so much. This is a serious job, and you'll need to tone it down and put up some boundaries. No more open door."

I rolled my eyes. We'd been talking about that door ever since I moved into the vice presidents' office suite. I had an open-door policy for anyone who wanted to drop in that her predecessor had loved, because he knew that visiting my office was the best way for him to get the scoop on things. But this woman . . . well, as I said, she cared about being *sophisticated*. She wanted to keep the executives closed off and private.

And then she hit the big one.

"You'll need to stop using words like 'blessed.' It's too churchy. You need to say 'lucky' instead."

That's where she lost me. Sure, the rest of it was unsolicited leadership coaching, but I would have considered some cosmetic changes. I was already skilled at the "code switch," leaving most of my colloquialisms and family stories about the projects at home and away from my mostly white workplace. But not saying "blessed"? She couldn't just start erasing words from my vocabulary. She couldn't erase the foundation I knew I stood on. I knew who I was and whose I was.

I politely thanked her for her time and then turned down the promotion.

Kenny's eyes were now huge, and he was practically jumping up and down. "I got a barber! You can be Cindy!"

No. I wanted the job, of course, but I didn't need it. I was already one of the highest-ranked women in a global company. I made more money than I'd ever dreamed of, and plenty to support my family. We had a good house. My mom had a good house. I loved my team and my job. I loved the company.

I was *blessed.*

My boss finally sounded happy. In fact, she was practically cooing with delight. "I agree with your decision," she said. "It's too much to ask you to fit the mold of an officer. You're smart, but you don't have what it takes for this." She assured me that she would smooth things over with her bosses and hung up.

I looked at Kenny. "Nineteen years ago I had to take off my red shoes and take down my braids. I'm not going to do that again. I've got to be me, and I am Cynt. Period."

⚭

After that conversation, I started to change my look. No, not the way that boss wanted. In fact, I went to the opposite. More bright colors. More patterns. Cheetah print was no longer out of the question. On casual days, I started rolling into work with my Berkeley sweats. Of course, I still wore AT&T blue—I'm always grateful to the company that helps me keep a roof over my family's heads—but that line between "home" and "work" styles started to fade.

These days, I love to make hashtags for things like the authenticity I discovered twenty years into my career. I always say it means #doyou.

"Do you" is a message I give my kids all the time. I've raised four authentic people who know and celebrate who they are. God made each of my kids wonderfully, and I make sure they know they don't need to let anything box them in or fundamentally change who they are.

Now, before you get the wrong idea, there's a caveat to that message. I actually tell my kids, "You do you . . . to a point." They also need to read a room, understand a culture, and above all, respect the other people around them, especially their bosses and their elders. Some people, they know, may not be able to handle all of them right on day 1. Sometimes a piece of them might need to stay in the car until they know the lay of the land.

But the thing I learned, and the thing I remind them, is that there's a difference between *moderating* who you are and *changing* who you are. I've always said that if I couldn't talk about the Lord at work, they could hand me a retirement check, but that doesn't mean I'm going around preaching and trying to baptize my co-workers. And if someone ever asks my kids, or the people who work for me, to compromise their integrity, or fundamentally change who they are, that's when they know they can calmly stand up and walk out and I'll have their backs 100 percent.

There's no job or relationship that's worth turning into someone you're not.

∞

I actually turned down four promotions over the course of my career, and each time it was because at some fundamental level the new job didn't feel like a good match for who I was as a person or what I wanted at the time. But the decision was never easy.

Let's be real. Nothing about being a woman in a male-dominated industry, or a Black person in a business dominated by white executives, is easy. I've dealt with people who think I'm fundamentally not as smart as them, not as talented as them, or not as worthy as them. I've mostly had amazing bosses, but there were a few over the course of my career who tried to shuffle me off to a corner where no one would see me. There were people who told me I should be home in the kitchen with my kids. More than once, some vendor or customer walking into our offices mistook me for an executive assistant.

There were people who couldn't believe that a woman—let alone a Black woman—was capable of being an effective, powerful executive. With every promotion, someone in my circle assumed I would fail.

And this isn't just something that happened "back then" and not today. When I got to my current job as CEO of the Dallas Mavericks, there was a person there who openly said, "Don't listen to her. She won't last ninety days." Four years later, I'm still here, and that person is not.

I've spent far too much of my professional time overcoming biases, proving that I'm honest, that I'm qualified, that I can do the job. I've learned to don my armor and let a lot of insensitive and downright hateful things slide off. But I've still brought my whole self to every job. And sometimes that paid off.

⬡

Kenny and I were still standing in the kitchen, a little in shock over the offer I'd just turned down, when my phone rang again.

"Cynt," said a male voice I recognized as our CEO, my boss's boss. I noticed that he put the emphasis on the *t* in my name.

"I just heard what happened," he told me. "Let's start this conversation again. The person the board of this corporation elected to be an officer is the same person whose office I sat in a few months ago."

"Yes, sir," I said. Did he have to go and bring up that office visit?

I'd been offsite, spending the day in meetings with our team in San Ramon. We were all in the conference room when someone pulled me out and told me Ed Whitacre was on the phone for me.

I was sure it was a joke. The chief executive officer of our enormous company based in Texas didn't know who I was, and he certainly wasn't calling me.

"No, Cynt," they said. "Ed Whitacre is in San Francisco today, and he's calling you. You need to run to the phone."

I went into a colleague's office, and they transferred the call. I could see right away that it was coming from my private office number. That was strange. When I picked up the phone, I heard, "Hello, this is Ed Whitacre."

The CEO was in my office? I just about died of embarrassment.

He'd flown in from the corporate headquarters in San Antonio that day for some event, and he popped into our office for a spontaneous visit. In hindsight, I realize he'd probably actually come by to meet me, because he knew that I was being considered as an officer, even if I didn't. At the time, though, I had no idea. I just knew that this brilliant, successful executive was in my office on a day when it was a mess. We were right in the middle of a big case, and our marathon sessions had left piles of papers and files everywhere.

I stumbled through a bunch of apologies. Ed was kind and encouraging. We hung up. And now here he was on the phone again.

"I've been in your office," he said again. "I've seen your sign that says, 'Lord, there's nothing that can happen here that You and I can't handle.' I saw the rock on your desk that says, 'I can do all things through Christ.' And I like that you're a praying woman. I want someone on the team who's praying us through all of this. So you go ahead and call yourself blessed, because that means we're blessed with you."

I was speechless.

"We selected you to be an officer just the way you are now, Cynt," he said. "You're the person who's getting everything done. I don't want you to change a thing. So let's start over."

He offered me the officer position, and I accepted. And I didn't change a thing.

21

Rethink What's Possible
(Round 8)

Wednesday, April 27, 2011, 8:54 A.M.

Good morning, my friends! Round 8 is underway at the Chemo Clubhouse. It's hard to believe that at the conclusion of this round we will be two-thirds of the way home. Your love and prayers have gotten us to this point!

Round 7 was brutal. Honestly, that's the only way to describe it. It was by far my roughest round, as the Oxaliplatin (a.k.a. "mean medicine") seemed to be working overtime. Several nights I slept on the bedroom floor, underneath the ceiling fan, just trying to get comfortable. But it was okay because one of our prayers during Round 7 was for me to stop working so much and get some rest. Well, because of weakness, fatigue, nausea and issues related to my central nervous system, I was able to get A LOT of rest. I couldn't do anything else for about five days. The Lord has a way of slowing me down by any means necessary and I was able to get plenty of sleep during Round 7.

In fact, in slowing me down, the Lord was not only refreshing my body, but saving our home from a garage fire. Last Tuesday evening I was resting quietly—enjoying the unusual absence of any noise in the house—when I heard two explosions. I made it downstairs in time to discover a full-blown fire in the garage, sparked by an exploded battery pack on an electric bike. I safely evacuated the house and called the fire department. More than twenty firemen were at our house in three minutes. It reminded me of the kind of rapid response that I've received from the Lord on so many occasions, especially since December. By the way, everyone is fine.

Over the last four months I have learned even more how to take EVERY need I have to the Lord. The following scripture, which many of you have sent me, has become ALIVE for me: "Now unto him that is able to do exceeding abundantly above all that we ask or think, according to the power that works in us . . ." (Ephesians 3:20).

I have given every physical, mental and spiritual need to the Lord, and His rapid response has been amazing and beyond my thinking. He has used so many of you as His messengers to deliver timely answers. Because of YOU my PMS (physical, mental and spiritual) health is better than most people expected at this point in the chemo regime.

In fact, physically I'm looking good with my new short hairdo—I mean really, REALLY short hair! I decided that I was no longer going to cover up the bald spots, nor was I going to continue to comb clumps of hair out of my scalp each day. So, the baby got the hair chopped off last week and is cute with a low maintenance crop Afro. My son's hair is actually longer than mine, and he has short hair. He's promised to show me how to get waves in my hair for my fancy "after five" look. All kidding aside, hair is the least of my worries. If I go bald, which is not anticipated with colon cancer treatments, I will slap the AT&T globe on one side of my head, a cross on the other side, and the words "Rethink Possible" spread across my forehead. Some are still wondering how I can be alive after having undetected cancer for two years, cancer in my lymph nodes and blood vessels—and now they can't find anything. "With God all things are possible" (Matthew 19:26). I rethink possible every day!

I am so grateful for all of your Easter wishes. I felt resurrected by Good Friday and was able to do all of our traditional things and even more. The Easter party at the Chemo Clubhouse was a HUGE hit and really lifted the spirits of everyone. I will start planning the May party very soon.

Thanks for all of your prayers for my family. Kenny and the kids are doing just fine. It's so wonderful for my kids to see the love of God in action on a daily basis. I love you and I appreciate everything you are doing to make this easier for The Marshalls. We are traveling on a wonderful journey and still picking up people along the way. Let's continue to pray for people who have been impacted by tornadoes and extreme weather. I also know of people who have been recently diagnosed with breast cancer who need the prayers of this powerful support team. I will be sharing some of the prayer blankets and hoping to make some house visits soon. In the meantime, I will be wrapped up in the prayer blankets that you've given me as we embrace the effects of Round 8. It's all worth it. I LOVE YOU!

Cynt

It's easy to get hung up on hair, especially if you're an American Black woman. When I was growing up, some of the girls and women in my neighborhood were getting perms, trying to have long, flowing hair that was more "white" and less natural. My parents were united in their opposition to that, though—not just because we didn't have the money, but because they wanted us kids to love the hair we had. I got my press and curl every year for Easter, but perms were out.

"Your nappy hair is beautiful," my father told us, and since we couldn't cross him, by the time we were teenagers, my brothers and sisters and I had turned our attention away from long and straight and instead set out to see who could make the biggest Afro.

That was my look when I went to Berkeley, to the fascination of all my white sorority sisters. They'd gather around me as I got my hot plate and comb, which I heated until smoke came off it, and then set to blowing out my hair and teasing it up, and out, and then up some more. I sprayed the whole thing with my beloved can of Aqua Net. Once it was set, that hair didn't move, even when I was moving all over the place as a cheerleader.

By the end of college, I'd traded the Afro for braids—at least until I got that job and *that* boss. Then, for almost thirty years, my hair was straight, shoulder-length, and *appropriate* for what everyone else wanted to see.

Then came cancer.

Ask people what they know about chemotherapy, and the first thing most of them will say is some version of "it makes your hair fall out." That's true—the poisons in some chemo cocktails can attack hair follicles, adding the insult of baldness to the injury of everything else that's happening. What I didn't know until I started my own cancer treatments is that not all chemo is the same when it comes to hair, and my specific cocktail wasn't likely to make all my hair fall out, but it would probably take some of it.

I'd heard plenty of stories by then about the emotionally devastating effects of cancer-related hair loss. I also got some good advice from my sister-in-law, Phyllis, who'd already been through her own cancer journey. She told me that one morning I would wake up and find a clump of hair on my pillow, or I'd comb my hair and find a clump of hair in the comb. That was the sign, she said, to call the barbershop right away and make an appointment to cut it all off. Don't wait for it to fall piece by piece, because each time that happened, it would hurt my soul. Out of everything she'd gone through with cancer, Phyllis said, watching her hair fall out was the hardest.

I figured I had enough going on without worrying about some kind of hair trauma. When I started to find those clumps of hair, just the way Phyllis told me I would, I called a barbershop where the stylists specialized in "chemo cuts" that protect a person's dignity and scalp. Not only that, but they refused to accept payment from clients with cancer.

As Kenny drove me to my appointment, I called Anthony, who was the most likely person to appreciate the thought of me in a barbershop chair.

∽

The first time we laid eyes on the little boy who would become our son, Kenny said, "All he needs is love and a haircut."

Kenny grew up in a family where the men kept their hair short and went to the barbershop every week, and he'd continued that tradition. Now here was this little guy with a bushy little Afro and a pitiful, sad expression. Just looking at two-year-old Anthony, you could tell he'd been neglected. Kenny watched him for a minute and nodded. "We've got the love, and I've got the haircut."

From then on, my husband and my son went together to the barber every week. As Anthony and his friends went through their teen years, Kenny and I sympathized with the parents of some of the kids who tried some crazy styles. All through high school, my boy kept it short and neat. Rebellion wasn't really Anthony's style.

When he went to college, things changed. Just a few weeks before my cancer diagnosis, he called one night and asked if he could get his hair cut into a Mohawk. Of course I said no. Our family has respectable, classic hair; I didn't want some Fro-hawk at my Thanksgiving table.

I was working out of AT&T's Charlotte office that week, and when I called Kenny that night, I told him about Anthony's request and my response.

My husband was quiet for a while.

"What's up?" I asked. "Something going on at home?"

"No," he said. "Something's going on on this phone."

That got my attention.

"We're not together on this one," he told me. "How old is that boy now? Eighteen? For as long as he's been with us, he's done everything we wanted him to. Gone to every church event. Played every sport, went to every camp, and worked with every tutor. In a roundabout way we even picked his friends. He's given us no disrespect, no talking back. Now he's eighteen years old and all he wants is to pick his own haircut? I say we should get out of the way and let him."

Kenny had a point, as he usually does when it comes to the kids. "But you're the one who's always big on the haircuts and the barbershop every week," I said.

"He'll still go to the barbershop," Kenny said. "He still needs his style. But let the boy choose his hair."

In other words, I needed to step back and let my son be himself. And that meant he was growing out a little Fro-hawk just at the time I was cutting off most of my hair. Just another example of how the Lord has a sense of humor. I called Anthony back and gave my blessing to whatever he wanted to do with his hair. I also told him he should thank his father for my new outlook.

The women cutting my hair in the barbershop were wonderfully gracious and kind. I told them I wanted a very, very small, cropped look that wouldn't make the bald spots as obvious. The stylist set about cutting almost a full head of hair off me, since I'd come after losing only a couple of clumps. I kept looking at it on the floor as she rubbed me on the back, asking if I was okay.

"I'm fine," I assured her. "It's just hair." And I meant it. Out of everything that happened in cancer, losing my hair was the thing that was easiest for me.

When I was done, I called Anthony again. "Well, it's official," I told him. "My hair's shorter than yours." Kenny, who was driving, cringed. For all of his support of the boy making his own choices, he really didn't like the Fro-hawk.

Anthony laughed and demanded that I take a selfie right then so he could post it online.

No, I said. I couldn't do that just yet. Facebook would have to wait.

My sweet son got quiet. "I get it, Mom," he said. Thinking I must be traumatized, he said he understood if I wasn't ready for people to see me without my normal look. He was precious in his empathy, but also totally wrong.

That wasn't it at all, I assured him. I look *good* with short hair. Turns out, I have the face and head shape for it. But my new haircut would look even better with big earrings, and I didn't have any with me. So I was on my way home to pull out the biggest pair of earrings I could find, and then I would send him a picture.

I was fine with how I looked. I just wanted to come out styling.

22

Know You Are Loved

The most important messages that you or I can give any child—especially an adopted child—are that they are loved and that they are wanted. Each time we added a child to the Marshall family, Kenny and I knew our primary job was to give them the stability, the security, and above all the *love* that they needed to find their ways through whatever had happened in their past and whatever would happen in their future.

After that, we helped them understand their place in the village, and that the Lord put us all on the earth to see about one another and take care of one another. When someone is sick, or is sad, or doesn't have something they need, we help. Period. And it's the responsibility of the adults of the village to care for the children, especially if someone's biological parents can't do it.

Or, as I told them when they were small, "big people take care of little people."

Anthony has always had a tender heart. At four years old, once he understood that he had a forever home, he was already looking for a way to share the love. It was only a few months after Kenny came home from the hospital that I found my little boy waiting for me by the door after work, excited and babbling something about a sister and calling "the hundred kinda" number.

I eventually worked out that he and Kenny had seen a feature on the local news about a little girl who was up for adoption. Anthony told his dad that she looked sad because she was so little and she needed a big brother to take care of her, and so he would adopt her just the way we'd adopted him. He said nothing about the girl needing a mom or dad, by the way. I'm not even sure we were part of his plan except to help dial the phone.

Every night he'd pray for the girl on TV whom he was going to adopt.

Kenny and I were ready to add to our family, too. We'd always planned to have a houseful of kids. So Kenny called the "hundred kinda number"—an 800 number, it turned out—and a few weeks later we met Shirley for the first time. She was two and a half, the same age that Anthony was when we first met him, and we realized that she was born the same month that we brought Anthony home with us.

The Lord was moving, gathering us together.

Shirley was born severely underweight and drug exposed. Her biological mother was a sex worker and addicted to cocaine, and she never sought medical care during her pregnancy. She showed up at the San Francisco General Hospital ER to give birth and then walked out of the door without her baby as soon as she could. I've thought about that a lot over the years, and my heart breaks to imagine how dire that new mother's situation must have felt for her to just walk away. I'm sure she loved her baby.

According to the hospital records we saw, the doctors all thought the newborn wouldn't survive with so many challenges, but our Shirley has never backed down from a challenge. Trust me on this.

She was in the hospital for weeks, then eventually discharged into the hands of a foster family who specialized in caring for special needs kids. She lived there for a year or so, until the family told social services that she was higher functioning than the other children in their custody and that she could probably be placed through the mainstream adoption system. Someone decided to feature her on the local news segment about children who needed homes, and the rest, as I say, is history.

Shirley was small for her age—even as an adult the girl barely tops five feet and weighs next to nothing—but from day 1 she met all of her brother's energy and love, and she gave it right back to him.

At Shirley's official adoption ceremony a few months after we brought her home, Anthony was front and center, as nervous and excited as I'd never seen him. "Order in the court!" he kept shouting. He quieted down when it was time for the ceremony, and he held Shirley's hand as we promised to love and commit to her. When it was done, he looked at the judge.

"So this is my sister?" he asked. The judge nodded.

"No one in white cars will come to get her?" The judge looked at us, and we whispered, "Social workers."

"No," she said. "No one's coming to get her. This is your sister forever."

I could see the tension just melt off him. "Thank you, JESUS! Now let's go to McDonald's!" he shouted, and still holding his sister's hand, he started to run in circles around the courtroom, whooping and hollering. The judge looked at us and shrugged and then gathered her robe and started running in circles with the kids, and then everyone else joined in.

❧

About the same time we brought Shirley home, we unexpectedly added a third child to our family.

Before we adopted Anthony, we read all of his case files, and the same question jumped out to both me and Kenny. "Where's his brother?" we asked, immediately and repeatedly. Rickey disappeared from Anthony's life as soon as the police found them in that hotel.

I think the caseworkers were concerned that having an older brother would discourage us from adopting our little boy, because they told us first that Rickey lived hours away, near Sacramento, and then that Rickey was a "bad actor" and would be a poor influence on Anthony. Neither, it turned out, was true.

When Anthony was almost five, his social worker notified us that his biological mother had passed away. She'd had AIDS, and the social worker wanted us to get Anthony tested (we did; he's fine). They also asked if we'd be willing to share photos of Anthony with Rickey, who was old enough to remember his mother and was really grieving her loss. In four years of separation, he'd never stopped asking about his baby brother, the caseworker admitted. They thought seeing Anthony might help him through this new loss.

That was the first time that we learned that Rickey wasn't in Sacramento. In fact, he was right around the corner from my mom's house in Richmond. Rickey, when he entered the child welfare system at nine years old, was considered too old to be adoptable, and so the state sent him to a group home. That could have been tragic, but Rickey's residence was run by a wonderful woman named Minnie who had a real gift for giving teenage boys a stable and loving home. Not only that, but he had just started high school at Kennedy High, where I had gone and where my mother now worked in the office.

We made a counteroffer to the social worker. Rickey could have all the pictures he wanted, but Kenny and I would bring them to him ourselves. If our meeting went well, we would reunite the brothers, which had been our hope all along. It had never sat well with us that those boys had been separated after everything they'd been through.

The meeting went better than well. Fourteen-year-old Rickey looked just like the little boy in our house, and he was overjoyed to see pictures of his brother. We sat with Minnie and cried as he went running off to show the pictures to the other boys in his house, because we could hear how much love and pride was in his voice.

Kenny and I both knew that we needed to bring these boys back into each other's lives, and with Minnie's blessing we took Rickey right over to where Anthony was having a playdate with a friend.

That morning, we'd told Anthony that we were going to go see his brother, but the word was foreign to him. "You mean he's like my cousin?" he asked. Between my siblings and Kenny's siblings, our son already had a bunch of cousins.

"Sure, honey. He's like a cousin," I told him.

"No," Kenny corrected me. "He's your brother."

Later, in the car, I asked what that was all about. The boy didn't know what a brother was, I tried to explain several times, and he didn't understand, so what difference did it make?

"It makes a big difference," Kenny said. Anthony wouldn't understand right away, but one day he would know that it was his brother who saved his life.

We called our friends who were taking care of Anthony and asked them to make sure that Anthony would be the one to open the door when we arrived. When he did, Kenny and I stepped back so the first person he saw was Rickey.

"You're my brother?" he asked, in that five-year-old voice that will melt your heart.

Rickey scooped him up and hugged him tight. He was crying. We were crying. The playdate parents were crying. The whole thing was beautiful.

From that moment forward, Rickey was part of our family. We offered to adopt him, but at fourteen he was comfortable at Minnie's house and in his school, and he didn't want to leave his foster family. "Do I have to choose?" he asked, and of course the answer was no. If there was ever a boy who deserved the love and support of two families, it was Rickey.

He came to our house on weekends and holidays, and in between he was always stopping in to the Kennedy High School office to get a hug or some extra lunch money from his new grandma. He immediately jumped into the lives of his new siblings, Shirley as much as Anthony. He was, and still is, the most patient and adored big brother imaginable.

Rickey is a part of every family meeting, every holiday, and every vacation, and today he calls me almost every day, just like the rest of them. The sibling bond is unbreakable, as if they had all been together in the same house from the beginning.

23

Focus on the Finish Line
(Round 9)

Wednesday, May 11, 2011, 11:34 A.M.

Greetings from the Chemo Clubhouse! Round 9 of chemo has begun, and there is light at the end of the tunnel. But it is *not* a train. It is the light of victory! Complete recovery is definitely in sight, thanks to all of your prayers and encouraging words. The Lord is touching and healing my body EVERY DAY!

The last round was a bit rough, but thankfully not as rough as it could have been. The Oxaliplatin "mean medicine" was left out of the last round because of the adverse effects on my Central Nervous System. I don't mind having to wear gloves and fluffy socks most of the time and I'm managing the hot flashes and the ever-increasing fatigue. Even the bone pain from the white blood cell booster shot is tolerable now. I've actually gotten used to the pain and see it as "things are really working." But, when I can't swallow and thus can't eat, my caregivers get concerned. So, they are continuing with the other two meds for this round and giving me a break from the "mean medicine" until Round 10. Of course, these two meds have their own bad side effects, so keep praying.

There are only three more rounds to go in this 12-round battle. Three-quarters of the race has been run and the finish line is in sight!

Over the past two weeks, I have been quite busy at work and at home. Although I had to spend most of the time in the hotel, I was able to travel in the car with my family to Winston-Salem for Shirley's dance competition, which was a mile away from where Ken Anthony attends college. I was feeling poorly but very happy that I was able to join in the family activities. Ken and I observed our 28th wedding anniversary, but we delayed celebrating until August when I have taste buds and lots of energy. Mother's Day weekend caught me feeling much better so I packed it with quite a few personal and work events.

I give God the credit for enabling me to do things despite my health challenges. People are still amazed at how well I look (even with the Teeny Weeny Afro) and how active I am and they wonder, "What kind of chemo and cancer is this?" Well, here's my secret: "The Lord is my light and my salvation; whom shall I fear? The Lord is the STRENGTH of my life; of whom shall I be afraid?" (Psalm 27:1). From the day I heard the cancer diagnosis, I was not afraid. I learned as a teenager that because I am a child of the King, "no weapon that is formed against me shall prosper" (Isaiah 54:17).

I have also gained strength every day from YOU. Your messages are incredibly encouraging. You make me laugh, cry and appreciate how wonderful it is to have so many friends who are taking the time to pray for me and reach out to me. I've been in the "connections" business for a long time—30 years on July 6th. Yet, I now really understand the true value of connecting with people. I have a new appreciation for "reach out and touch." You have touched me with your words, flowers, fluffy socks, calls, cards, emails, food, prayer blankets, pearls, weekly prayer circles, books, visits, BIG earrings and unique gifts. I opened a card last week that included cutouts of the AT&T globe, a cross and the words "Rethink Possible." One of my dear work Sisters read my last journal entry and couldn't resist sending me the cutouts in case I go bald. I laughed out loud for hours. I've decided that some of you are as crazy as I am.

Well, they are getting ready to hook me up to Winston (my chemo pump boyfriend) for the next three days. Poor Winston, I have him into everything. He can't keep up with me. But just like Kenny, Winston lets me think that I'm in charge. But truly, Winston is in charge and is being used to save my life. And, YOU are also being used to lift me and my family in prayer, encourage my spirit and save my life. I love and appreciate you very much!

Cynt

From the very first day I went to chemo, I insisted that everyone around me continue their lives as much as possible. I wanted my kids to stay in all of their activities. I wanted my co-workers to charge forward with our agenda. No one, I decided, should skip a beat while I handled this temporary cancer setback.

Those were the right things to want, but there were unexpected consequences for me. It killed me to be laid out at home while Shirley was off doing dance recitals. I knew that Kenny was there and that she and her dad were bonding in important ways while they drove around. I wanted that for them, and yet I also wanted to be there. My poor husband wasn't sure what to do. I wouldn't let him cancel any of their events, but then I'd be upset when they'd call me from the road, reminding me of everything I was missing while I lay there on the sofa, feeling my body change. I was used to being on the go all the time, and it was a consistent struggle to accept that being still was the most important task I had right then.

Not that I had much of a choice. Chemo took such a toll that being more involved was almost impossible. There were some days when I felt lethargic to the point where I could barely put one foot in front of the other. Walking was difficult. Moving swiftly was unheard of. That really played on me mentally because it reminded me of just one more thing that cancer had taken from me. No one had to tell me to slow down. My ability to move quickly and outpace most people had been replaced with shortness-of-breath slothfulness that I had rarely experienced.

And then there was what happened to my mind.

∽

I'd first heard about "chemo brain," the mental cloudiness and memory lapses that most cancer patients experience to some degree, in my pre-chemo research. Dr. Eisenbeis told me that I should expect to feel some level of cloudiness. But like all of the other effects of chemotherapy I was sure I could avoid, I brushed off the warnings. I was entirely focused on the finish line, the time when I would be cancer-free.

Remember Gary, the survivor who'd told me about the waves of exhaustion? Well, he'd also told me about chemo brain. He warned me that after his first few rounds of chemo, he couldn't remember certain things. "Don't get upset when the same thing happens to you," he advised, "because it happens to everyone." The only recourse was to laugh it off and even use it when convenient.

At that, I laughed openly. "Gary, my memory is my secret weapon. I can remember what socks you wore in a meeting we had ten years ago, and I know EVERYTHING you said. Memory loss, please!" Kenny agreed. He calls it my "total recall" memory and says it often works against him.

Then, a few rounds into my chemo, Shirley came into my bedroom to check on me on one of the "bad" days, when I was in a lot of pain from the white blood cell booster shots. Those things were always brutal; for a day or two after, I hurt all the way to my bones.

But the pain wasn't what made me burst into tears when I saw her.

She rushed over and asked what was wrong. My strong-willed girl had finally decided I wasn't going to die, but I got the feeling she could change her mind again at any moment.

Finally, I confessed I couldn't remember her name. "I have it," I sobbed. "I have it. It is actually happening to me. I have chemo brain. I don't know your name."

A little forgetfulness wasn't as bad as the things Shirley had probably imagined, and so she rolled with it. She patted me on top of the head, told me not to worry, and then got very close to me, forcing eye-to-eye contact. "I'm Shirley," she said, and then she repeated it a few more times for good measure.

After that, Shirley made it her job to make sure I remembered every person who came over, whether I needed it or not. "Mom, Auntie Yvonne is here. Auntie YVONNE. YVONNE from college. Auntie YVONNE. Come on in, Auntie. It's YVONNE, Mom. YVONNE. Your friend YVONNE!"

It was cute at first, and we all laughed at the way Shirley was showing up for me. I had to calm her down, though, when she started shouting the names of foods and other things. The girl thought I had complete memory loss.

Ten years later and with my memory fully restored, I'll still sometimes have some fun and ask her, "Who are you?"

Every time, she'll yell at the top of her lungs, "I'M SHIRLEY!"

24

Show Up

The message "you are worthy of love, and you are worthy of being cared for" is powerful. I've seen how, if someone feels as if they came into the world unloved or unwanted, that can mess them up for life. The stable, permanent love of other people is one of the things that gives us confidence in ourselves and a sense of community with others, and that's true for adults as well as children.

Kenny and I were both working high-pressure jobs in downtown San Francisco when Anthony and Shirley were small, commuting every day from our home across the bay. It was a tough schedule, but we were committed to giving our children a stable home and managed to coordinate our calendars so that someone was with them as much as possible.

When Anthony and Shirley were in elementary school, one night everything just went sideways. We both got stuck at work and couldn't get back across the bridge to pick up the kids from their after-school care on time. By the time I got there, all of the lights in the building were off, and I could just make out two little sets of eyes walking toward me down the dark school hallway, followed by one not-so-happy teacher stuck after hours.

Our kids all came to us with some abandonment issues, and so I could see that to them this wasn't just a story about Mom and Dad being stuck at work. This was another abandonment. They were traumatized.

That night I looked at Kenny and said, "The Lord did not bless us to adopt these kids so that the daycare can raise them." He agreed. We knew one of us needed to quit working in the city to be here more for the kids.

Kenny didn't hesitate. "Well, I guess the W-2s speak for themselves," he said lightly. He had a good job in IT, but my becoming an officer at Pacific Bell came with a paycheck neither of us could quite get used to. "I'll quit tomorrow."

And he did. For a while, he continued to work from home while also juggling after-school practices and tutoring and playdates. After about a year of that, though, I came home one night to find his office empty. Kenny and the kids were in the kitchen, rocking out to loud music and wearing matching aprons. Shirley was sitting on the counter, and Anthony was standing next to his dad, chopping up olives.

Kenny told me that after all the running around from school to tutoring to practice, he'd gone back to his desk to finish up "just a few things." The kids kept coming to the door to ask about dinner. "Dad, we're huuuuungry."

It was seven o'clock before he really heard them, and that's when he realized that the kids were the reason he'd started working from home and not in the city, but ignoring them at home was no better than leaving them at daycare.

He turned away from his computer. "What do you want to make for dinner?" he asked, and they picked enchiladas. They went to the store, came home, and put on the music, and that's where I found them. And it was beautiful.

Kenny calls it the night he crossed over. To this day I don't know if he ever quit that work-from-home job, or if they eventually fired him, but it didn't matter because the kids were his primary focus from then on.

Years later, a California reporter asked him what it was like to be a stay-at-home dad. Was it hard for him to quit his job while his wife brought home a paycheck? My husband didn't hesitate. "A real man will do whatever it takes for his family to thrive," he told her.

∽

That's not to say that I didn't still feel the pressure of being an executive and a mom.

I'm often asked how, as a mother and executive, I managed my "work-life balance." I always say that I didn't balance. I'm not sure I even believe that balance is possible. Instead, I tell them that I always strive for integration, bringing my whole self to both my office and my family. And I bring my family to my work.

When Anthony was in the fourth grade, he was really excited about his classroom Halloween party. When my boy is excited, I'm excited, so I got the whole family a themed set of 1970s costumes—I still remember Kenny's had a giant red Afro wig and vest and a big medallion—and made arrangements to take part of the day off from work so that I could be there, too.

Then my boss's boss announced he wanted me to present at the big annual town hall meeting. He specifically asked for me because he needed to keep the energy up during the meeting, and he knew I was lively and could get a crowd engaged.

Of course the town hall was scheduled for Halloween morning.

I made some adjustments to my plan. The town hall was first thing in the morning, so I told the organizers as long as I was done by 10:30, I could put on my costume at work, drive straight to the school, and still be on time for the party.

Of course the program got delayed.

I was bouncing in my heels all morning, just sick about how I couldn't leave, and how I needed to get to my boy's party. This was a big deal for him. I knew Kenny was already there. All of the other parents were there. I'd promised to be there.

Finally, I did my thing and got off the stage, but I was *late*—way too late to even change into my Halloween costume. I tore out of the parking lot, raced thirty minutes to the school, and practically sprinted into the classroom where the party was in full progress. I stood in the doorway, in my corporate business suit, looking at a roomful of parents and kids in full costumes. I felt just awful. If you've ever tried to juggle kids and jobs, you've probably been there with me. I was in tears but trying to hold it together as I reluctantly entered the classroom.

Anthony saw me come in and rushed over to me, and all of his little buddies followed him. For some reason, all of those sugar-high kids zeroed in on my ID badge still clipped to my jacket.

"Look, everybody," said Anthony. "My mom's dressed up like a *worker*. She looks like someone who works for the phone company." He went on to make up all kinds of half-crazy stories about what I did, based on the conversations he overheard in the car and his own imagination.

The other kids jumped in and started asking me dozens of questions about the badge. How could they get one like it, and what kinds of doors did it open, and did other badges have different colors? I could feel the other parents—the ones who'd spent hours working out every detail of their costumes and snacks—start to steam a little, and I wanted to tell them that I had worked on a costume, too. I'd tried to fit the party plan. But in the end, the most important thing wasn't what I was wearing; it's that I was here in this room with my son.

I realized that day that my presence mattered more than some kind of self-imposed expectation about how I thought our time together should happen. It wasn't about the perfectly baked cookies, or whether I stopped at the airport gift shop to buy a present on the way home, or what other parents thought about me.

The most important thing I could do is show up.

The most important thing any of us can do is show up.

25

It's Gonna Be Okay
(Round 10)

Tuesday, May 24, 2011

Pre-Summer greetings from the Chemo Clubhouse! I'm throwing our monthly party today to celebrate life and the blessing of excellent healthcare. When I look around the Clubhouse today I see God's healing power at work. I know the club members—while weak and physically challenged—are all alive because Jesus said he came "that they might have life, and that they might have [it] more abundantly" (John 10:10). So many of you have reminded me of the earthly and eternal abundant life that has been promised to me.

We are celebrating LIFE today with some summer fun and BBQ in the Clubhouse! These people will miss the party planner in July. Well, maybe one man won't miss me quite as much. During the last round I must have been talking too much and having too much fun (imagine that) when he wanted to be grumpy. He remarked loudly to his wife that it "used to be quiet in here." Well, you know I just couldn't let that go—so I politely invited him into the conversation! And I let him know that Love and Happiness are present in the Clubhouse on the days I'm at bat. I also reminded him of the new game plan we established in January: we "party and rejoice" while we are in the Clubhouse. He's now my new best friend and thanked me when he left. His wife winked at me and told me that's just what he needed. I'm waiting for him to come in now so I can put a lei on him and give him some BBQ ribs. We have to eat while we are here because we may not be able to eat for a week once they finish with us!

Round #10 is underway and I expect it will be a difficult treatment. The Oxaliplatin (aka "mean medicine") has been added back to the chemo regimen. While the side effects from the last two rounds were significant, it's always more challenging when all three chemo meds are administered. I am blessed, though, because studies show that the "mean medicine" only needs to be administered in half of the treatments in order to get the job done. And guess what? Out of nine rounds the Oxaliplatin has been administered five times so far. This round will be the sixth and final round for this mean medicine. So while I'm already feeling neuropathy (high sensitivity to cold, inability to swallow, etc.) I am thankful for this powerful medicine that works to improve relapse-free survival. I plan on being an alumna of the Clubhouse very soon and remaining in that status for the rest of my life. So I welcome the Oxaliplatin and the difficult week ahead.

I am so grateful for all of your prayers and support during Round 9. It was a very busy two weeks filled with some great work activity and some fun stuff at home. Last week I represented the company in my first and second official speaking engagements this year, successfully worked on another big policy issue, coordinated a birthday party, hosted fourteen teenagers and their parents for prom pictures and parents party, then went to church with my family on Sunday morning and unexpectedly hosted some folks for Sunday afternoon fun. Needless to say, I'm a bit exhausted starting Round 10, but it felt so good to be almost normal the past few days. The bone pain and fatigue tried to keep me down but they lost. The Lord gave me strength to do everything I wanted to do to keep my life moving.

The kids are wrapping up the school year over the next two weeks so I'm a bit concerned about my energy level during this typically busy time of year. Kenny will be helping Ken Anthony move out of the dorm on Thursday and I'm excited about having the boy home for the summer. By the way, Ken Anthony got a tattoo on his arm last Friday that reads "It's Gonna Be Okay." This is the song he wrote when he heard about mom (me) having cancer. The song is also now the theme song for a local talk show. Good things (the song and sentiment, not the tattoo) continue to come out of this situation. It reminds me of the scripture that reads "In all things God works for the good of those who love Him, who have been called according to His purpose" (Romans 8:28). I've watched my children become more dependent on God and their faith in Him has increased. Honestly, I'd go through this again for that outcome alone.

You have no idea how much your expressions of love mean to me. Your weekly chats with God, companionship during my treatments, fluffy socks, food, cards, calls, yo-yo toys, assistance at work, home-made bread, flowers, See's candy and other goodies are so encouraging. One of my buddies in Dallas recently sent me a stuffed monkey with a card telling me to tell Winston (my chemo pump) that soon he will not be the monkey on my back. The note is too funny and the monkey is very cute. Another of my company girlfriends—blessed with a sense of humor and the right "app"—sent me a photo of herself in a "temporary bald moment" as an expression of solidarity.

I am in awe of your love and my spirits are high. Each round causes more fatigue and pain but it only makes me more determined to beat this disease. It also makes me pray for the thousands of cancer patients who are fighting this battle around the country.

Well, the BBQ is waiting, so let me close with this story: the prom teenagers (none were Marshall teenagers) at our house Saturday were all wearing a blue ribbon on their gown or tuxedo. I didn't ask about the ribbons, but was quite curious since I like to know everything. I was struck by the beautiful "Cal" blue color of the ribbons and by the fact that all 14 of these wonderful young people were obviously bound together by some type of cause. Well, just before they boarded the limousine, they lined up with each holding a poster board that all together spelled out "Thank you so much." One of them then mentioned what they thought I already knew: the blue ribbon is the symbol for colon cancer. I just wept. These youngsters, like all of you, are praying for me and keeping me close to their heart. I am so blessed.

Nine rounds down, one underway and two to go! I LOVE YOU.

Cynt

That last round of the Mean O left me in a fetal position on the floor. I couldn't eat. I couldn't move. I was grateful, knowing I was so close to the finish line, but I was so sick that I thought I might just lie right there for the whole two weeks.

But when the president of the United States calls, you get up off the floor and carry on with your life. There are some things that you just do no matter how you feel.

～

The first time I met Barack Obama, it was 2008, and he was a young Black senator from Illinois running an upstart campaign to be president.

I was at a meeting in Greensboro when Venessa called to say Obama had a campaign event in Charlotte that afternoon and they'd invited me to come as a VIP guest and sit in the front row for his speech. A local businessperson would even send a car for me, if necessary.

Going to political events wasn't unusual for me by that point. Influencing public policy that benefited AT&T was a big part of my job, and that meant meeting and lobbying politicians from every party. On behalf of my employer, I donated to candidates and attended both the Democratic and the Republican National Conventions every four years.

I learned years ago that to be effective in my job, I had to avoid favoring red or blue. I wasn't hung up on Democrat, Republican, independent, or anything else. I was blessed to work with business friendly, community-focused, civic-minded, consumer-oriented policy makers. We cared for the citizens of North Carolina.

In 2008, Obama's campaign was historic and especially momentous for people who looked like me. I stuck with my general philosophy of staying neutral relative to my job and politics, but being asked to attend Barack Obama's event was different. I'll admit that this moment felt special.

I agreed to attend and arranged for Venessa and another member of my AT&T team to meet me there. Greensboro is about one hundred miles from Charlotte, so it was a long ride. By the time we got to the venue, I could see lines of people stretching for what seemed like miles, waiting to get in. Obama wasn't president yet, but he was already a very big deal. I called Venessa to let her know I'd arrived but would probably be standing in line for a while. She told me the campaign staff wanted me to come right to the front door, because they needed to get the VIP guests checked in and settled before they opened the event to the public.

Well, that didn't sit right with me. I told my chief of staff I wasn't going to cut off all these people who were waiting in the sun for hours. I would stand in line with everyone else, and I'd get in whenever I got in. But it turned out the decision wasn't up to me. As soon as the car stopped, a couple of Secret Service agents opened the doors, and they almost picked me up as they hustled me right past all of the people and into the air-conditioned building, where my team was waiting.

They took us to our seats in the front row, and someone from the campaign told us that after the speech Senator Obama would come around and greet us each individually.

Suddenly I was nervous.

I thought about all of those people outside and all of the people watching us live on TV. I thought about Birmingham, and the 16th Street Baptist Church, and Dr. King. I thought about the possibility of a Black president.

It all seemed so crazy, so I did what I always do when things get crazy. I called my mother.

"I don't know what to say when he comes over," I told my mother as I waited for the event to start. "Maybe I should ask to pray for him."

"Of course you should," she told me.

Obama gave a great speech, of course. Whatever your politics might be, it's hard to deny that he's a phenomenal orator. After the event, I watched him make his way down the front row, pausing to greet each person, and I could feel my hands getting moist, my mouth became dry, and I became a bit light-headed. I wasn't quite at the fainting phase, because I didn't want to miss him.

When Senator Obama got to me, he smiled. "It's so nice to meet you, Madam President." That's what he called me. His advance team was incredible, if they could prep him like that for every person in the line.

I was still having a case of nerves, so I just blurted, "Can I pray for you?"

He smiled and said he'd like that, so I grabbed his hands and we bowed our heads. And this is where I messed up, because I hadn't really thought past that moment, and I had no idea what to say next.

One of my go-to Scripture verses for prayer is from the book of Isaiah, where it says, "No weapon that is formed against you shall prosper." I love the idea that the Lord creates a shield that deflects whatever's coming, even if we don't know what it is. And so I prayed the words of Isaiah over Barack Obama. Or at least I tried to. As soon as I got to the word "weapon," every Secret Service member standing near us leaped forward and grabbed their own weapons . . . the real kind.

My eyes popped open. Obama's eyes popped open. The security men's eyes were already wide open, looking everywhere for this "weapon" threat.

"Oops, sorry about that," I said. "Wrong verse for this crowd."

We both had a good laugh, and the Secret Service settled back down when they realized I was just praying. I offered a generic, nonviolent prayer of blessing before Senator Obama continued down the line of people, and I made my way out of the event center to get to a speaking commitment of my own that night.

I was already driving away when Venessa called me to say that after the crowd thinned out, Obama asked to speak with me again. He genuinely wanted someone to pray the words of Isaiah over him. But I was already gone, and I couldn't disappoint the ballroom full of women waiting to hear me speak, even if it was for the future president of the United States.

"Tell him I'll catch him next time," I told her.

～∞～

The "next time" turned out to be during my chemo. President Obama was coming to Durham to promote his Council on Jobs and Competitiveness, and as the chair of the North Carolina Chamber of Commerce, I was part of the small group of local leaders invited to meet with him after the public event.

It was the fourth day of my tenth chemo round, and while I'd returned Winston to the Cancer Centers of North Carolina, I was in rough shape. Still, I got myself off the floor. When the neuropathy in my fingers made it impossible to handle the zipper, my friend Jackie came over to help me get into my good yellow suit—the one that fit again because of the weight I'd lost. Off I went to meet the president of the United States, even as I wondered how I was going to pull it off. I was so doggone sick and fatigued I could barely walk, and the summer heat was almost unbearable. Chemo had made me unexpectedly incredibly sensitive to temperature changes. In the winter I could never get warm enough, and now with summer approaching, I couldn't get cool enough. The neuropathy prevented me from being able to drink or touch anything cold. It seemed impossible to find relief from the blazing-hot weather.

This time, I didn't make a fuss about wanting to stand in long lines or wait my turn to get in. If I was going to attend at all, I needed to get in and out quickly. I gratefully accepted every accommodation that my staff and the Secret Service arranged. The car dropped me right at a door, and Venessa and an Obama staff member got me to my seat, where they'd arranged for fans to blow right on me to keep me cool and to fend off the nausea.

Once again, when the speech ended, I stayed put and waited for President Obama to approach me. Would he even remember me? It had been a while, and I didn't look like the person he'd met just a few years before. My appearance had changed so much that I'd started to tell my staff to warn people about the effects of my chemo before I met them in person. I wasn't embarrassed by it, but I didn't want them to be shocked, and I definitely didn't want their pity. If this was how I needed to look in order to be alive to meet them again next year, then it was fine.

I swayed as I stood there, dizzy and skinny, my skin several shades darker from the chemo drugs. I knew I didn't just look *different;* I looked *bad.* I looked sick.

But it was clear that once again his advance staff had prepared him, and he approached me with a smile of recognition.

"How are you doing, Mr. President?" I asked, just trying to keep my head up and eyes open. I wasn't up for a Secret Service–challenging prayer this time.

"Madam President, I think I'm doing better than you." He reached out and held my hand. "You're in my prayers."

How the tables were turned, along with the prayers. But in those moments, I was grateful that I'd made the effort. For a few minutes, life continued on, and cancer didn't exist.

26

Don't Do Life Alone

I was just three months old when my parents left Birmingham, and we never had the money to go back to visit when I was growing up. I'd been a Californian my whole life. But the lessons of the South were ingrained in me in ways I never realized.

Not long after we moved to North Carolina, I was invited to lunch with the former governor Jim Hunt in his office. It was just the two of us, but his staff had arranged a fancy table spread with white linen. "Southern hospitality," he said with a flourish.

We chatted for a while before he told me why he'd called. "I've been tasked with getting to the bottom of a mystery," he said. "Everyone who's met you comes to me and says, 'Where's she really from?' We don't believe you're from California. You're too nice."

I laughed and told him that I was a little offended by that, because there were plenty of nice people in California, and assured him I'd lived there my whole life. I was a California girl through and through. But he kept digging, until he finally asked where I was born. I told him about being born in Birmingham and leaving when I was three months old.

The governor slapped his hand on the table and grinned. "I knew it!" he said. "News flash, you were raised by Southern parents. That makes you Southern." And he was right. I never considered myself a Southerner, but a few people who knew what a Birmingham accent sounded like had told me they could pick it up in my voice. Then, when I came to North Carolina—my first immersion in the South—the hospitality and community always felt like home to me. I fit there. I fell in love with the South, and thank the Lord, the South returned all that love to me and my family.

≈

Being an officer of a communications company that was steadily buying up other companies meant that I was always on call to help navigate another merger. I'd been moving up the ranks in California, doing some high-profile projects for the company, and by the time Anthony and Shirley were approaching their teenage years, Kenny and I knew that I could get "the call" at any time.

"The call" was the invitation—they called it an invitation, but it was really a directive—to pack up and move to a new state, to take over as an executive of the company that had been bought. When AT&T bought out BellSouth in 2006, we needed new leadership teams in possibly nine different states, and so I had a hunch that it was my turn.

On December 29, Shirley's twelfth birthday, our family was at a Golden State Warriors game when the phone rang. I was outside the arena when I took it.

When I got back to our seats, Kenny looked at me. "What happened? You look like you've seen a ghost."

I looked around at the stadium and thought about the Bay Area that was so familiar to me. California was all I knew. It's where I'd lived my whole life, shy of three months. "I got the call," I told him.

Kenny started to smile. He's always told people that from the time we got married, he just strapped in and stayed open to whatever crazy thing happened next. "Where are we going?"

"North Carolina."

❮❯

I had to do some negotiating with the merger team, because, though I accepted the job and agreed to start right away, I also explained that meant they needed to move my whole family within the next three weeks.

"It's school break for the holidays," I explained, "so we need to get them settled in time to start back with the rest of the kids in January." Anthony had just started high school and Shirley was in her first year of middle school, already new schools for both of them, so the timing was perfect. They had missed only one semester of school with their new schoolmates and had plenty of time to make friends before the summer.

My merger liaison suggested that there wasn't a rush. Most AT&T executives go ahead to get settled into their jobs, he explained, while their families stay home and move the following summer.

Most AT&T executives, I pointed out, were men. This mama wasn't going to leave two kids for that long. My family needed to come with me.

The merger team made it work. They got our house packed, our belongings moved, and a temporary living situation all lined up for us. Before we had time to really know what was happening, the kids and I were sitting on the floor of an overcrowded JFK airport on a layover, waiting to go to a state we knew nothing about.

"Mom, do they have hurricanes in North Carolina?" Shirley asked in a small voice.

"Baby, they're going to have two just as soon as we get there, because we are going to take over this place." I smiled, trying to be reassuring, but the kids were pretty shell-shocked. To make it worse, their dad wasn't even with us. Kenny had gotten sick right before we left, and his doctors advised that he wait another day or two before he got on a plane. So it was just the three of us Marshalls who landed in Raleigh late one winter night and took a car to a furnished apartment that would be home for a few months while our own house was being built.

It was a lot to put on my family. It was a lot to put on me, too. Taking over a whole statewide operation, without knowing the players, was hard. Doing it right after a merger that had eliminated the jobs of many of the previous leaders, and likely left some hard feelings, was *really* hard. I didn't know the customer base, or the legislators, or the regulators in North Carolina. I didn't even know the geography. For the first time in my life, I let my boss talk me into hiring a driver to take me to work functions, mostly so that I wouldn't get lost and show up hours late. I quickly figured out that it was worth it, because it allowed me to focus on the work, rather than directions.

I hit the ground running, bouncing back and forth from my office in Raleigh to AT&T headquarters in Charlotte from my first day. I made friends. I built relationships. I put things back in order. It was exhausting, but it also felt right. North Carolina felt right. The Lord had chosen me, a Southerner who never knew she was Southern, and put me in the best place in the world for the things that would come next.

Not only that, but He put the best people all around me.

∽

You've already heard about my posse of North Carolina friends, who surrounded me with love and laughter throughout my chemo. Now let me tell you about how the Lord brought them into my life at just the right time.

I'd met Hokey back in California, when she worked as a nurse with my sister-in-law. We became close, talking almost every day, and stayed in touch when she decided to leave the Bay Area and move back to Raleigh to be near her big extended family. In fact, the only time I'd ever visited North Carolina before we moved there was when Kenny and I flew to Raleigh to be in Hokey's wedding.

The day I called her to say that I was being transferred not just to her state but to her city, she screamed so loud I could have heard her across the country even without the phone. She set us up with a Realtor and helped us find a place to live just a mile up the street from where she and her daughter Ashley lived. Anthony and Shirley, who had worried about moving away from their aunts and uncles and cousins, discovered they had an instant family waiting in their new home. And I had a friend who was ready and willing to show me the ropes.

Then, a few weeks after we arrived in Raleigh, I was at an event for local leaders when I thought I recognized the profile of a woman walking by. I'd known Yvonne even longer than I'd known Hokey. She was my best friend in college and a bridesmaid in my wedding. We'd drifted apart after that, though, and I had no idea she'd left California. But that woman walking by sure looked like Yvonne.

The people at my table—including the then-mayor of Raleigh—laughed at me. There was no way my best friend from the University of California, Berkeley, three thousand miles away, would just *happen* to be at a community breakfast in North Carolina, almost thirty years later.

When the familiar-looking woman walked past me a second time, I decided to follow her. The people at my table shook their heads and talked about how embarrassed I would be when it wasn't her. But when I reached the woman and really looked at her, and she looked at me, we both screamed. (Screaming is a common reaction among my friends, I'm noticing.)

Yvonne and I picked up right where we left off. She came to

my house that night and showed my kids pictures of me as a college cheerleader, with my giant Afro and tiny waist. She was wild and used language in my house that my kids could never get away with. Of course they loved her immediately.

I introduced Hokey and Yvonne, and they became best friends. And at the same time, Anthony was making friends at church, and we did a lot of stuff with their parents. That's how I met Bev and Lisa, who fit right into our group. Almost overnight, we became the posse. I had lots of acquaintances all over the state of North Carolina because of my job, but these were the women who knew the real me and whom I knew I could trust with anything. Even my life.

27

Learn from the Journey (Round 11)

Tuesday, June 7, 2011

Greetings from the Clubhouse! Round 11 is underway at the Cancer Centers of North Carolina. This is my next to last chemo treatment and I am very excited. I'm reminded of the scripture, "Weeping may endure for a night, but joy comes in the morning" (Psalm 30:5). My morning is almost here!

The last two weeks were mixed with difficulty and happiness. As expected, my doctor added the "mean medicine" back into the chemo regimen for Round 10—and the Oxaliplatin was meaner than ever. I had to talk to it a few times as I was throwing up or laid out on the floor in pain and experiencing hot flashes. The inability to swallow and sensitivity to cold were especially difficult. Just imagine 97 degree weather and not being able to comfortably sit in an air conditioned room or drink a cold beverage. So, I put on my chemo pearls, gloves, and fluffy socks and made it through some rough days and nights. (Of course everything was color coordinated and I looked like a diva grizzly bear.) Thanks to your prayers and God's amazing grace I made it to much better days by the end of the round.

Last week, we had a fun time celebrating the high school graduation of my best friend's daughter, Meka. My 16-year-old daughter, Shirley, provided much joy during her end-of-year dance recital. And on Sunday, June 5th, we cried while watching Ken Anthony on the keyboard praising the Lord with the Sunday morning worship team, and then celebrated his 19th birthday! Not to mention the joy we felt when we learned that our youngest daughter, Alicia (13) aced her end-of-grade exams and will be moved out of her middle school special education classes into regular classes in the fall. So, even with the mean medicine trying to upset things, it didn't work.

Great things are still happening in my life and I'm thankful every day for the strength to carry on with my mommy duties.

I've also been able to continue working . . . probably much more than most people realize. It's just in my bones and I can't help it. It's also my way of letting this cancer demon know that it cannot take any aspect of my life. "I can do all things through Christ who strengthens me" (Philippians 4:13). Fortunately, I have a great work team and a wonderful buddy, Sylvia, who are supporting me in a way that is simply heart-warming and unselfish. Not to mention the daily support that I'm getting from all of you in a variety of ways.

By the way, someone anonymously sent me a big "church lady" hat. It is simply beautiful. I am indeed a church lady and I LOVE big hats. One time when riding to church Kenny told me to take off my hat and put it in the trunk with the spare tire. It was just that big and he couldn't see around it. So "thank you" to whoever sent me the hat. It is coming in handy during these very hot North Carolina days. Apparently, chemo meds don't mix well with the sun. I learned that the hard way on Memorial Day. So now, I'm sporting my big hats when necessary.

Here it is—the moment I've been looking forward to for four months, since Round 3. You know I skipped the fifth grade and I've always been considered pretty smart. Yet, I still have a lot to learn. The Lord used this cancer opportunity to show Ms. Cynt a few things. So here are some of my key learnings from this remarkable journey.

Things I've taken for granted
1. Drinking a cold glass of water.
2. Walking barefoot on a cold floor.
3. Smelling food.
4. Taste buds.
5. Energy!
6. Fighting off a cold.
7. Hugging people without getting sick.
8. Strength to pray and worship.
9. Ability to swallow.
10. A terrific memory.
11. Working at a wildly fun pace.
12. And. . . . I can't remember the last one! I know I had twelve. Chemo brain!

Things I've now learned to love and appreciate
1. Navy bean soup.
2. Red grapes.
3. Blueberries.
4. Mango.
5. Daily call from my mother in California.

6. Exercise power walking.
7. Daily interference in my daughters' lives.
8. Intimacy with my Savior.
9. Waiting on God to order my steps.
10. "919 Dine" food delivery service.

Friends, my prayer over the next two weeks is for the Lord to give me strength to do some things that He clearly directed me to do at the beginning of this journey. He slowed me down for a reason. There are some things I need to do and some big decisions I need to make. I want to hear His voice clearly. I'm also praying for all of you who voluntarily jumped on this journey with me. Many of you have had your own trials arise over the past few months, but you stayed on the journey with me and I will always be grateful.

After this round we only have one more to go. I'm looking forward to June 23rd when we will walk out of the Clubhouse untethered by Winston and I will have my groove back.

I LOVE and APPRECIATE YOU!

Cynt

"Handle your business." I've said that to my kids so often they can see it coming now and shoot it back at me as soon as I open my mouth.

My kids' business—even when I had cancer—was to go to school and focus on their education. My mother had instilled the value of education in me, and I wanted to share that with my children. Shirley and Alicia didn't get free passes out of class or their after-school activities just because I was in chemo, and I finally had to tell Anthony to stop coming home from college every weekend just to check on me. He had business to attend to at school, and watching his mother sleep on the couch wasn't getting that done.

My business, they knew, was AT&T.

It's probably obvious to you now that my career has never been just a job to clock in and out from, and that was especially true when we were in North Carolina. Being the president of AT&T in the ninth most populous state in the country meant that from the minute I arrived, I'd worked like a dog. For four years, I never stopped, never turned it off.

My office was in Raleigh, the state capital, where I worked closely with the legislators and regulators who affected our policies. Almost every Monday morning I'd catch a seven-thirty train to Charlotte, where AT&T had its state headquarters office. I'd meet with the staff and stakeholders there for a couple of days, then take the train back home on Wednesday to be in the Raleigh office for the second half of the week, and with my family on the weekend. I took every Sunday morning off to go to church, and as often as possible I set aside Friday nights for family nights, but I still worked seven days a week. Investing in people during the day meant that I usually had piles of paperwork to do at night, and then there were the breakfast meetings, dinner meetings, evening committee meetings, and community events all over the state. I was always running from one place to another and one meeting to the next. I was always on call (on an AT&T phone, of course). I loved every minute of it, but it was a lot.

To this day, my chief of staff from that time, Venessa, tells me that our crazy pace, ripping and running from city to city and meeting to meeting, aggravated my body past its limit and let the cancer grow. I don't know that there's science behind that, but her words still hit me, because all of that stress couldn't have been good for whatever was inside me. Sooner or later, something was going to have to give, and in my case it had been my colon.

I was loyal and committed to the company that had built my career, and by and large it really was an incredible, supportive, and inspiring place to work. But like any huge organization or group of people, there were pockets of resistance and challenges that tested my resolve.

I had just gotten home from a round of chemo with the Mean O and all of its aftereffects. Kenny dropped me off, and then, thinking I'd just go upstairs to sleep, he zipped back out to pick up groceries. I wasn't in bed yet, though, when I heard the doorbell. Had Kenny forgotten his keys? I made my way slowly back down the stairs and opened the front door, only to find two women I didn't know.

One of them introduced herself. "You don't know me," she added. I nodded. Even with chemo brain, I knew that I had never seen this woman before.

She went on to say that she worked for the State of North Carolina and that someone from the internal affairs office of AT&T had called her more than once. Then they'd flown all the way from Atlanta just to show up at her workplace, asking a lot of questions about me. She said she told them we'd never met, and she felt like they didn't believe her. The woman went on to share more details of their conversation.

I stood there perplexed. I wondered if these were the same auditors who I had visited with on my birthday. They had asked a lot of questions about our North Carolina operation.

"I didn't want to come today," the woman said. "I've seen the newspapers. I know you're going through cancer, but I live in the neighborhood and didn't know any other way to reach you. After the men came to the office, though, my boss said that something didn't feel right and I needed to let you know what was happening. I hope I didn't catch you on a bad day."

I thought about the chemo chair I'd just left and Winston strapped to my hip. My physical sickness was bad enough, but what I was hearing filled me with an emotional sickness. Still, I told her, "Keep going." This was important.

She told me that she came because she was offended, both as a Black woman and as a Christian, that people kept treating her like a liar, and probably treating me the same way. "There's a witch hunt against you," she concluded. I leaned against the door and listened.

Corporate politics can be messy, I knew that. Audits are common, and putting up with them is part of being an executive. As I've said before, my experience with AT&T was excellent overall, but there are, and will always be, individual people who are suspicious of others who succeed. I'd been working long enough to understand that it wasn't my job to carry their baggage, but after the women left my house that day, I still picked up the phone and started making some calls. My heart was as broken as my body, but my integrity was at stake, and I wasn't going to let a little chemo sickness stop me. It was time to handle my business.

I wished that I didn't feel like I had to fight cancer and an audit at the same time. I'd been riding the corporate roller coaster of promotions and setbacks for thirty years. I was eligible for a pension, and I had a lot of other things that I wanted to do with my life. Was this a sign that it was time to retire? Kenny thought so. He told me over and over to let it go. No job was worth crawling and bleeding my way up the stairs the way I had just days after surgery, or forcing myself onto the phone just hours after chemo. He never believed that answering their questions would change anything. I always believed that the truth would prevail, and it did, eventually. I had faith in my company.

As I reflect, I believe there was a message in the timing of the end-of-year, routine audit and battling cancer. I wonder if that moment was really the right time to handle my work business. Some things don't matter as much when your life is at stake. The unfortunate timing of that conversation with the women at my front door drained the mental and physical energy that I needed right then to fight cancer. My bosses heaped me with praise for how I handled things. Of course, everything came out just fine, and by the time I returned to work, it was as if the whole thing had never happened.

$$\approx$$

This particular unexpected and unpleasant situation at work sticks in my memory today partly because it was the exception in my experience of having cancer, not the rule. I cannot say often enough how much the people around me blessed me during those darkest times.

When I moved to North Carolina, one of the first meetings I scheduled was with the Reverend William Barber, at the time the head of the state's NAACP. On the day of our meeting, he called his counterpart in California and said he was on his way to have lunch with the new president of AT&T North Carolina, to "straighten her out and tell her how things are done here." I'd gotten the job after a merger that generated some hard feelings and a lot of suspicion across the state, and Reverend Barber wasn't the only Southerner wary of a California executive.

He asked his California colleague, a woman I'd worked with extensively over the years, for any information she had about me. The woman laughed. "I could tell you a lot about Cynt Marshall," she said, "but I think I'll let you just go to that meeting and see for yourself. Call me when you get back."

Those were the days before it was popular to just google someone or check their LinkedIn picture, and so Reverend Barber came to the meeting with no idea I was a Black woman. He actually walked right past my table in the restaurant, scanning the room for someone he thought looked like what he expected. I had to call him back, and when he saw me, I could see he was taken aback. When he sat down, he was still cautious, but I could see he was ready to change his own perspective.

Then it came out that we were both from Apostolic church backgrounds, and he loosened right up. We sat there for three hours and had loud and crazy church right there in the restaurant.

Fast-forward to my year of cancer and chemo, and one day I was at home, sicker than ever. I couldn't even make it upstairs to my bedroom, so I was lying on the couch, fading in and out of sleep, when Alicia came to find me.

"There's a really big man at the door," she told me. "He said the Lord told him to come and he needs to see you, just for a minute. I told him you were sick, and he says you don't have to talk. He just needs to see you."

Well, if the Lord sent him, I wasn't going to argue. Alicia helped me to the door, and I realized the "really big man" was Reverend Barber.

He gently told me that he had a revelation from the Lord that morning that I was not having a good day, and so he'd called Venessa and badgered her into giving up my home address. Then he recruited a volunteer to drive him an hour and a half from his house to mine, just so he could pray for me in my presence.

He laid his hand on me, closed his eyes, and prayed. When he was done, I thanked him. I was still sick and weak, but suddenly had enough strength to get up the stairs to my own bed.

28

It Takes a Village

Not long after we moved to North Carolina, I had a meeting in Charlotte with the Children's Home Society of North Carolina, a beautiful organization that helps kids in need of a family find forever homes.

Well, as you've seen, the Lord has given me a lot of blessings, and it's my opinion that my task is to find the best ways to give those things back through my time, my talent, and my treasure.

Ever since we adopted Anthony, I'd volunteered and supported programs that provided permanence and stability for kids, and we'd arrived just as the Children's Home Society of North Carolina was launching a big campaign across the state. They wanted AT&T to be a sponsor, but more important, they wanted me to be on their board. I was impressed with their pitch and asked for a few days to think about it.

I went back home, and the first night that we sat down to dinner, fifteen-year-old Anthony jumped in. "Mom, do you know how many foster kids there are in the state of North Carolina?"

I told him that actually, I did know that, because of my meeting. "But how do you know that?" I asked him.

He started to tell me about a special he'd seen on TV while I was gone.

"Oh, not the TV again." I smiled and put my head down, but he kept going, telling me about a piece on the local news, produced by none other than the Children's Home Society of North Carolina. There was a brother and sister on the TV special, he told me, and he just knew those were the next kids we were meant to bring home.

"You said we'd adopt again when Shirley was a teenager," he reminded us.

He had us there. Kenny and I had always told the kids that we wanted to adopt again. We talked about how as a family we were equipped to bring in older kids this time, the ones most at risk of getting lost in the system. But I didn't want to displace Shirley's role as the youngest too soon, and so we'd talked, generally, about waiting until she was a teenager. Now her thirteenth birthday was rapidly approaching, although with the move and the new job Kenny and I hadn't been watching the clock. Anthony, on the other hand, had been.

I tried to tell him that this wasn't the right time to make a decision like that. We needed to get settled in North Carolina before we could think about bringing someone new into our family. We were still living in an apartment while our house was being built, and we didn't have room for more kids. I was still getting used to this new and very big job. I threw every excuse at him that I could, but they all came down to the same thing. I just didn't think I had enough time.

But Anthony was insistent. The boy and girl he saw on TV were the ones, he said.

His description made me pull out the files from my meeting, and he flipped through the booklet of stories until he found the pictures of the kids he'd seen on TV. "It's a sign, Mom," he said. "A sign from God."

Once again, Anthony started to pray every night for the girl and boy he saw on TV. That weekend, when we went to look at the construction progress on our house, he and Shirley ran through it, counting bedrooms. "We have enough room," he announced breathlessly, "to adopt two extra kids and still have room for both our grandmas and Gran Gran to visit." My mother and mother-in-law were sure to visit, I knew. Although my father-in-law didn't travel, my optimistic boy always believed he could persuade his grandfather to visit us in North Carolina. He wanted to make sure we had room for them and his new brother and sister.

That boy is persistent, and his love is contagious. I looked at the Children's Home Society file again. The kids were ten and twelve years old, and it looked as if they'd never experienced permanence or stability in their family life. Alicia and her biological brother had bounced back and forth between their biological mother and foster homes for years, never knowing how long they could call any place home. Their mother had only recently relinquished custody.

It took several more months before I finally called the social worker assigned to their case. Yes, the kids were still in foster care and available for adoption, she said. Summer was fast approaching, and in the next school year they would be in the sixth and eighth grades.

That's when I knew for sure the Lord was calling us to grow our family again.

You see, Shirley was in her last year in middle school and would go to the same high school as her brother the following year, and I'd decided that we could handle adopting two kids in middle school. I already had the middle school schedule worked into my routine—the back-to-school nights, the first and last days of school, and when report cards came out. Instead of one kid in middle school and one in high school, we'd have two in each, but nothing would really change.

∞

In my almost thirty years as a parent, and my forty years as an employee, I've had to adjust to a lot of schedule changes and conflicting priorities. I've learned to separate things into what's truly important, what I call the crystal balls, and everything else, which I call the rubber balls.

Rubber balls bounce back to you if you drop them—or better yet, they bounce off to another person. Crystal balls, though, are the ones that leave shattered glass on the floor. If they break, you don't get them back.

The decisions about what's crystal and what's rubber aren't the same in every family, and sometimes they're not the same from year to year. For most of our kids' growing-up years, though, sports practices and car pools were rubber. If I wasn't there, someone else could do them.

But church on Sunday? That's crystal for me.

Meeting one-on-one with every employee when I take a new position? Crystal.

The first two days of school, the last day of school, and back-to-school night were also crystal, because my kids needed to see I valued their education. Sports games and dance recitals were crystal for many years. I maybe didn't stand by the door holding a basket the way my mother had, waiting for report cards to be dropped in, but I marked my calendar with the days that grades came out, and we always made something special out of it.

I've left a conference midday and flown home on my own dime to watch an afternoon swim meet and then flown back to the conference, because at the time, games and meets and tournaments were crystal for my kids. They really wanted to see Mom there, even if I was running in with my hair on fire and a briefcase still in my hand.

∞

You see where this is going, right? This was another one of those times when the Lord looked on my plans and smiled . . . and then brought His own plans to my attention.

Sometimes He's here to meet my needs. Sometimes He puts me in a place so that I can meet the needs of someone else.

The adoption process went smoothly, right up to the morning we finally met the kids in person and Alicia corrected the social worker. "Miss Jenny, I'm not going into sixth grade. I'm a year behind, remember, so I'll be in fifth grade next year."

Hold on, there. Fifth grade was still elementary school. Fifth grade would mean having kids at *three* different schools, not two. Fifth grade added another whole set of crystal balls to my already full hands.

This was not my plan.

My shock showed on my face—Kenny told me later it looked as if I had a heart attack right there at the breakfast table—and Alicia caught it. She was sitting next to me, and she turned her big, serious dark eyes up to me. "Is that okay, Mom? Are you still going to adopt us?"

Well, what could I say to that?

"Of course we are, baby," I said. "Of course we are."

I thought fast, and explained that the elementary school in our neighborhood was just at the end of our cul-de-sac, and so it was actually great, because she'd be able to walk to school every day. Over pancakes, I found myself shifting my expectations about sticking with old routines. This was a child who'd never had routines and desperately needed them, and big people take care of little people no matter what.

The Lord, as always, knew more than I did, and His plan was the perfect plan. Both kids came home with us, but before long we realized that Alicia's biological brother was not a good fit for Alicia or the family. So Alicia stayed with us, and he was subsequently placed with another family.

Alicia became our North Carolina baby, and we all poured our love into her. She was cautious with us at first, feeling out where she belonged. Trust was hard for her to give, and love was hard to receive. It still is. But we continued to remind her she was our only native Southerner, the real deal, and we needed her to help us settle in. Her new siblings loved her completely, and she fell into a routine and relationship with them first and most deeply. It was hard to remember the time when she wasn't part of our family.

Still, though, when Anthony went to college more than a year later, I told him to give me the remote control. "No more picking sisters off the television," I joked.

29

Be Grateful
(Round 12)

Thursday, June 23, 2011, 10:41 A.M.

Final Greetings . . . yes, say it with me . . . "FINAL" greetings from the Chemo Clubhouse! Today, I am wrapping up my 12th and last round of chemotherapy. Although I'm experiencing the usual chemo side effects, I'm feeling very encouraged and reflecting on one of my favorite scriptures, "But they that wait upon the Lord shall renew their strength; they shall mount up with wings as eagles; they shall run, and not be weary; and they shall walk, and not faint" (Isaiah 40:31). We've waited and now we are mounting up!

Round 11 was, as some had predicted, another challenging round (even without the mean medicine). The fatigue and nausea worked the baby into a fetal position for a couple of days. I found the most comfort when lying on the bedroom floor under the ceiling fan, with the air conditioner on 73, adorned in guess what . . . fluffy socks and gloves.

Lena Horne said, "It's not the load that breaks you down, it's the way you carry it." So, I'm trying to carry my load in style—matching socks, gloves and big earrings—and without complaining or asking "why me?" I already know "why me." The Lord wanted a vessel that would glorify Him while battling cancer. He wanted a vessel that would glorify Him while simultaneously fighting other battles. On December 30th, when I told my mother about the diagnosis, the first words she uttered were, "This is for His glory." I pray every day to be worthy of having been selected as one of His chosen vessels for 2011.

I can't begin to thank all of you for joining and enduring this challenging journey with me. It's as if we have been in the boxing ring for six months, not knowing exactly who or what we would have to fight in the next round, but always checking in with the coaches and trainers in the corner for support and strength. All of my family members, friends, and work colleagues (internal to AT&T and external) have made me feel like I am the most loved person on the planet. Thousands of cards, several face-to-face visits, hundreds of Caring Bridge postings and emails and hundreds of love gifts have shown me first hand that you really do "reap what you sow" (Galatians 6:7–8). YOU know how to encourage someone through one of the most difficult experiences of their lives. And, I say "one of the most" because this cancer episode doesn't quite rank up there with the 1994 death of Special K (our six month old daughter) but it has been quite painful and challenging nonetheless. However, because of my prior experiences with heartache, pain and suffering and the fact that God has ALWAYS brought me through each situation victoriously, I knew this battle would also be won.

I am walking out of the Cancer Centers of North Carolina in just a few minutes. In 30 days, the medical professionals will conduct a full body scan to ensure that there is no more cancer present in my body. Well, as the song goes, "Don't wait 'til the battle is over, you can shout now." I'm saying HALLELUJAH and thanking the Lord right now for being cancer free (as indicated by my last scan). Stage 3 colon cancer met its match!

I've had tremendous medical care throughout this journey. Thank you, Dr. Charlie Eisenbeis, for taking such good care of me. You are a great oncologist and a fine human being. A special thanks to "the Clubhouse girlfriends," the nurses and staff. I will always love you for the caring and compassionate way that you administered treatment. I will not, however, miss you sticking that big needle in my surgically implanted arm port. Okay, I know you gave me lidocaine and I finally used it to numb the port area. Well, you tricked me and took blood out of one of my veins instead of the port. I was trying to get a step ahead of you. You ladies are true professionals and a blessing to many.

To my new clubhouse team members who are also now sporting the blue colon cancer ribbon with me . . . I LOVE YOU! And remember, what happens at the Clubhouse stays at the Clubhouse—sort of like Las Vegas, but with much higher stakes on the table. Our conversations and parties are wonderful memories. I would say I'm sorry I made so much noise, but you wouldn't believe me and I'm not sorry. You needed to be awakened. We are alive! Maybe not always well, but we are alive. I will miss all of you at the Chemo Clubhouse. However, don't take it personally but I do not plan on coming back anytime soon. I have served my purpose at the Clubhouse and after our BBQ party today, I am kicking Winston (my chemo pump) and cancer to the curb!

Peace out, Winston. I've got to get on about my Father's

business in some new capacity. I am not sure exactly what that will be. But I am sure that God is up to something good and I'm ready!

At 51 years old, I'm thankful for a great family life. Kenny and the kids have been troopers. Kenny is used to going on wild "life" rides with me and has learned to take care of me while also holding on for the ride. I made a great decision 28 years ago when I said "I do." He didn't know I meant "I do plan on taking you with me wherever the Lord leads us . . . joyously up the mountain AND painfully in the valley." Ken Anthony, Shirley and Allie now know beyond question that we serve a true and living God who can still heal and deliver.

I'm also blessed to have made a great employment decision 30 years ago. I like to say I am ATT . . . Anointed To Testify. I'm in the right company. And by the way, to those AT&T employees who sometimes wonder about the human side of our big company, let me just share that our Chairman, Randall Stephenson, and one of his direct reports, Jim Cicconi, called me the very day they learned of my cancer diagnosis. Bill Blase's call soon followed when he received the news, as did the wonderfully heartfelt prayer from Cathy Coughlin. They offered to do "whatever" was necessary to get me the very best healthcare in the country. They, along with almost all of Randall's direct reports and several of my officer colleagues, continued to call and check on me regularly.

It is easy to return to work full-time, despite whatever else might be going on, when you work for compassionate corporate senior leaders like these. They really do care about us as individuals, as well as about us as company team members. While the cancer was the main entree on my plate—and more than "enough to say Grace over"—some very trying work challenges made for an unappetizing side dish. But God's amazing grace and the knowledge that this company is filled with loving people at ALL levels kept me sane on the work front. From the security guard to the Chairman, the genuine support has been overwhelming. THANK YOU!

Thanks to ALL of my family and friends who carried a spiritual weapon and cared for me during this battle. I appreciate each of you more than you can know. I can't name all of you, but I do want to send a special "shout out" to a few:

♥ My BFFs, Hokey and Yvonne, have done everything—from getting on my nerves by insisting that I eat blueberries, to making me laugh and cry while watching old classic movies.—I had actually forgotten about "What ever happened to Baby Jane." I guess they were trying to scare the cancer away that night.—Not a day went by without one of these women showing up to do "something" for my family.

♥ I'm also reminded of Venessa and Sylvia on Team AT&T, who I spoke to almost every day, and Clifton, who prayed like Paul and voluntarily, on his own time, reviewed my journal updates. Rob, Carlos, Herb, Connie and John also supported me in so many different ways.

♥ My mother, sisters, brothers, nieces and nephews wrapped me up in love and tears from Day 1 of this journey.

♥ Robin, your weekly chats with God meant the world to me. Keep talking to Him. Oh yes, I figured out that you sent me the church lady hat. It's beautiful and much needed in sunny, hot North Carolina.

♥ Jo Anne, you've started something with the fluffy socks.

♥ Carol, I will be incorporating frosting cupcakes in my annual family traditions.

♥ Sarah, my buddy who took me to many of my treatments and then sat with me through the process.

♥ Both Rick Smiths—the one who sat with me during my chemo treatments and the one from WRAL who gave this issue some press life.

♥ Patrick and Micki, thank you so much for coordinating the food and wonderful AT&T support.

♥ Several state and federal policy makers from around the country for their various demonstrations of love.

♥ Lori Ann and Fassil, your scripture readings were a daily blessing and constant encouragement.

♥ My Triangle neighbors—especially Jo Anne S, Patty B, Bill C, Jim K and Dianna—who brought hams, home-made bread, shepherd's pie and other dishes that put us in touch with new cultures.

♥ Lo and Sylvia, I cherish the angels that you gave me even before I began my chemo treatments. They have watched over me during the good days and the not-so-good days.

Again, this is just the beginning of the list. I could name a thousand wonderful people whose gestures are engraved in my heart. But I just don't have time. I gotta blow this joint.

Finally, my church family is amazing. I love the folks at Crosspointe Church, who decided early on that "food" was needed . . . lots of food! We've eaten well. Even when I couldn't eat, Kenny would close me up in the bedroom so I couldn't smell the food and then I would just hear bags being torn open. It was a blessing to not have to worry about this daily activity that I used to take for granted. My California, North Carolina, Texas and other friends went above and beyond to make life easy for us. I love you dearly!

So, I'm walking out of the Chemo Clubhouse right now, free of Winston; free of a return appointment and free of the White Blood Cell booster shot that prepares one for the next chemo round. There is no "next" round. I suspect that I will endure a week of side effects but that's perfectly fine with me. My comforting prayer blankets and pearls await (thank you Julia, Tracy, Janet, Amy, Vivian, Patty and so many others).

I will send all of you the "official" good news after my

scan in 30 days. I know I am cancer free and soon the doctor will have evidence that confirms this fact. Let me close with how we began this journey when I heard these words on the other end of the phone the day before New Year's eve: "Cynthia, I have news . . . it's bad and it's significant. You have colon cancer and unfortunately, it's in your lymph nodes and blood vessels. This is not what I expected. Without chemotherapy you have a 25 percent chance of being here five years from now and it might be even worse." My immediate response was found in Psalm 91, the Psalm of protection: "He that dwells in the secret place of the most High shall abide under the shadow of the Almighty. I will say of the Lord, He is my refuge and my fortress: my God; in Him will I trust" (Psalm 91:1–2). "With long life will I satisfy him, and show him my salvation" (Psalm 91:16).

Thank you for loving me and my family. YOU and God's sufficient grace (thanks Brooks and Vicki) got me to this point. I will continue to pray for all of you as we pray for others who are battling cancer and other unique life challenges. This is one powerful prayer team! Adios from the Chemo Clubhouse!

Cynt

When it was finally June 23, I was *ready*. I wore some cute purple capri pants and a little white top that looked good with my big earrings and short hair. It didn't matter that my body was weak. I couldn't stop smiling. I knew in my heart that the cancer was already gone, that it was never coming back, and that this was truly the final round.

I had won the fight for my life, and June 23 was the start of my victory party. The Clubhouse party we threw that day was one for the record books, full of music, dancing, and hugs all around. It was beautiful.

Of course, I finished chemo the way I started, with my friends and family arguing about who would get to accompany me to the Clubhouse one last time. Eventually, Kenny, Yvonne, Hokey, and Bev piled into the car and took turns sitting by my chair.

Round 12 was still a full round of chemo, which meant I left that afternoon with Winston plugged into my port, pumping those nasty chemicals into me. Two days later, I dragged myself back to have him removed for the final time. We threw another party. And then, when I came back a month later for blood work and scans—the ones that showed everyone else that I was right and the cancer was gone—we threw a third party.

After that, as planned, I never went back.

Colorectal cancer like mine has a high recurrence rate in the first year, and so Dr. Tyner was hesitant when I told them I wanted my port taken out right away. A lot of patients keep their ports for a year after they finish chemo so that if the cancer comes back, they won't need to go through another surgery to implant a new one.

I knew my cancer was gone for good, though. It had done what it needed to do in my life. I agreed to leave the port alone for a few weeks, until those thirty-day scans showed no signs of cancer, but then I insisted it was time to move on. The port had to go.

It wasn't going in the trash, though. You'd think that by this point Dr. Tyner would have been used to my plans and ideas, but he still got a funny look on his face when he held up the plastic tube that had lived in my body for months and I told him it couldn't go into the hazardous waste container. He needed to sterilize it and put it in a bag or cup for me.

"I paid for it," I reminded him. "Willis is mine."

Yes, the port had a name. If my chemo pump was Winston, I'd decided that my lifesaving port was Willis, the little brother. Winston was a big machine with a big job, and when I released him after our twelve rounds together, I prayed over him and sent him off to help someone else.

But Willis? I explained to Dr. Tyner that I had other plans for him.

30

Take Responsibility

Dr. Eisenbeis had asked the question almost in passing during one of our early meetings. "There's no colon cancer in your family, right?" He had my paperwork in front of him, so he knew that on all of the family history forms I always checked no. But this time, when he said it, something clicked.

"Well, my father died last year," I said. "We think it was colon cancer."

My oncologist just raised an eyebrow.

"We were estranged," I told him. "He's not part of me."

❧

In the summer of 2009, my sisters Ros and Cassandra called to tell me our father was dying.

I already knew he was sick. I hadn't spoken to him directly for years, but Ros had always stayed in touch with him, and my brothers visited every now and then. Through them I'd hear what he was doing, how he was living. It was rarely good. There was one awkward day when I'd driven my mother to a VA hospital where he was a patient; she wanted to go, and I'm ride or die for my mama. He was clearly sick, but he was cagey with us about what was wrong with him. I hadn't asked many questions.

A few months before, though, he'd called me out of the blue. He wouldn't tell me what was wrong with him, but he just said he was sick. He apologized for a lot of the things that had happened and the things that he had said. I accepted his apology, but the door to having a real relationship had closed a long time before.

We hadn't talked again after that call.

I asked Cassandra if I should fly to California to be with them. No, she told me, the end was close. He'd refused chemotherapy, and the cancer had eaten him up. It was just a matter of days until the end, so I should just plan to come to the funeral.

A few days later, she called to tell me he was gone.

∼

When I told my kids I was going to my father's funeral, they had a lot of questions. I hadn't gone into many details with them about my childhood, but they knew why my father wasn't in their lives. So they rightfully wanted to know, why would I go all the way to California for the funeral if he was so mean? If he'd hurt their grandma so much and broken my nose? Shirley, in particular, was offended.

They were good questions. I told them I wasn't going to my dad's funeral for his sake. I was going for theirs. For as long as they'd been in our family, Kenny and I had taught them the Bible verse that says, "Honor your father and your mother, that your days might be longer upon the earth," which is something my mother also pressed on her own kids. No matter how bad my father was, we weren't allowed to speak disrespectfully to him or about him in her presence. We could tell the truth, but even after the divorce and that terrible summer of 1975 she wouldn't tolerate us bad-mouthing him, just as Kenny and I wouldn't tolerate our kids bad-mouthing us or their birth mothers.

∾

All of our kids know their adoption stories. They each know that we chose them to be part of our family, and that makes them pretty special. But they also know as much as we can find out about their birth families.

Rickey and Alicia were both old enough when we met them to have their own impressions of their biological families. But Kenny and I have told Anthony and Shirley everything that we know, and we're open with all our kids about the addictions and difficulties their birth mothers faced.

We didn't do it to keep them away from drugs and alcohol (although it turned out to be an added benefit; Shirley, especially, spent most of her adolescent years being very vocal about *never* trying any kind of drug because of what had happened to her mother). Instead, I always thought it was important for my kids to know that they not only are loved now but have *always* been loved, even before they came to us. I wanted them to feel confident that their birth mothers loved them, even if they couldn't care for them.

Because of things that had happened before my kids were born, mostly around drugs and alcohol, the women who gave birth to them couldn't keep their families together. They couldn't take care of themselves, let alone children, and so they were separated from their babies. But that doesn't mean their mothers didn't love them, and it doesn't mean that those women aren't also worthy of being treated with the respect a parent is due.

∾

Going to my father's funeral was a way to show my kids what it means to respect a parent, no matter what happened and what they've done. I wanted them to have that example. It was also a way to acknowledge that I could control only my end of the relationship, and to connect with my extended family, who had all been touched in one way or another by William Smith.

"But he was mean," Shirley said.

I couldn't argue with that. But I knew there was always a bigger story being told. "He was," I told her, because I don't lie to my kids. "But sometimes only the Lord knows what was going on in him. All I know is the Lord chose this man to be my father, and the rest isn't for me to judge. So I have to go to California."

Kenny stayed home with the kids. My mom, wisely, chose not to attend. And so when I went to the funeral home early on the morning of the service, I was by myself.

The funeral director was a guy I'd gone to high school with but hadn't seen in a long time. Chuck and I had a good chat and caught up, and then I side-eyed the casket.

"Is he really in there?" I asked.

Chuck just laughed, but he knew what I meant.

"I'm serious," I told him. "My daddy was a hustler; he always had a game. He's the kind of person who might not really be dead. He might be in the witness protection program or something." *Where did that come from?* I guess some part of me still held on to that scared-to-death child, and she was worried that William Smith might start popping up again.

Chuck nodded. "I wondered the same thing. I checked. He's in there."

"Show me," I told him.

And while it was probably breaking some kind of funeral home law or protocol, Chuck did just that. I saw with my own two eyes that my father was dead. He was never coming back.

❧

Except he did come back in that tumor in my colon.

I hadn't asked many questions about what killed my father. I'd assumed that his death came from the hard life he'd lived. The alcohol. The drugs. The running around on the streets. I'd stayed away from those things, and so I assumed I would also stay away from any consequences he faced.

But cancer doesn't work like that. The research says that as much as one-third of the risk of colon cancer is tied to genetics, and no matter how much distance I put between my father's lifestyle and mine, I couldn't just ignore my own genes.

My ignorance put my siblings and me in a dangerous spot. None of us had recognized that our father's early death might tell us something about our own health. When I got sick, we were all in our late forties and early fifties, prime ages for getting screened for colon cancer, but none of us had done it. None of us had even considered that we were in a high-risk category because of him.

Cancer, I finally realized, didn't care what kind of man my father was. It lived far deeper than that, in my very genes. So I started making phone calls, and within a few weeks all five of my siblings had colonoscopies. Thank the Lord, none of them had anything more serious than a polyp.

31

Find the "CAN" in Cancer

July 21, 2011, 4:16 P.M.

HALLELUJAH!!!! The CT scan results are in. . . . I am cancer free!

As the song says, "God did this thing." Thank you for all of your prayers. From the beginning we all focused on the "Can" in Cancer. Yes, He "can" heal me from cancer, and He did! I will go in for surgery tomorrow to have the chemo port removed from my arm since I don't need it anymore. I will visit with my doctors every 3 months over the next year and do everything I need to do to prevent this disease from re-turning. And, I will keep praying for all of you . . . my journey buddies.

"Weeping may endure for a night, but joy comes in the morning" (Psalm 30:5). It's morning my friends! This is the beginning of the second half of my life. My mid-life crisis is over! :-)

THANK YOU . . . THANK YOU . . . THANK YOU for being on this journey with me! We have beat cancer!

Remember, handle your medical business and get a co-lonoscopy. I love you!

Every year, as I mentioned, my girlfriends and I go to the Bahamas for a ladies-only getaway. We'd postponed it because of my chemo, but by the end of June it was obvious that I needed a trip that year, and beyond that I needed more than our usual rest and relaxation. This was going to be the ultimate end-of-cancer party, and Willis was the centerpiece.

I kept him close to me as we gathered ten divas deep—my posse, of course, and my youngest sister, Ros, my niece Gynelle, Venessa, and a couple of additional friends—in the airport. I kept him right in my carry-on tote bag as we noisily made our way through security and boarded our flight. That ended up starting quite a conversation with the airport security people, but I wasn't going to risk Willis getting lost. And there was no official rule about not bringing silicone medical devices onto airplanes. It was strange, but no one could come up with a reason why it wasn't allowed.

We were an excited, noisy, joy-filled bunch when we arrived at our resort in the Bahamas, and we attracted attention. My posse—especially Yvonne—told other people at the hotel about our plans for Willis, and everyone loved it. They all wanted to get in on the action. We'd only been there a couple of hours before random strangers started coming up and asking if they could come to the party.

So one afternoon, a few dozen people all got onto the hotel's excursion boat, which usually takes guests across the bay to fish or kayak or whatever. On that day, no one got off. Even the people who thought they were going on a day trip decided to post-pone their plans when they heard the DJ start to play Gloria Gaynor's "I Will Survive" over the speakers. Dozens of people were dancing and posing for pictures and having a good time. I didn't know most of them, but they were all there for me and for Willis. One by one, they came up and told me about their own encounters with cancer, and celebrated with me, and I heard my mother's voice, telling me again how my cancer journey would inspire people.

Once we were out in the deeper water, my little group gathered on the deck and had a ceremony of sorts. I said a prayer, and everyone shared their favorite stories about this cancer journey we'd been on together. Yvonne was glad to be done with the masks and gloves every time she came to my house. We all gave Hokey a hard time about her nasty-tasting smoothies. Gynelle laughed about the time she called me on day two.

And then I took Willis, wrapped in his little cup, and threw him into the ocean, saying goodbye to cancer forever.

32

Plans Change

With cancer behind me, Sylvia relinquished my office and I went back to work. My hair grew back. My kids got used to not counting on someone else to pay for their food deliveries. The Marshalls still enjoyed the hospitality of North Carolina, but people weren't in our house at all hours anymore. We put away the gloves and masks, and I went back to church.

In other words, life in Marshall Manor started to shift from crisis mode to something resembling our new normal.

It wasn't the same as before, though. A person doesn't go through something life-threatening and come out unchanged. But in many cases—and in my case—the new normal was better in a lot of ways.

For starters, I finally got the message and slowed down my hair-on-fire pace at work. I was thrilled to step back into my full-time role as the president of AT&T North Carolina just in time to start planning for AT&T's role at the 2012 Democratic National

Convention, which would be in Charlotte, but I never went back to the same crazy weekly travel schedule. The folks in the Charlotte office had done just fine without me being there three days a week, I realized. To be honest, I don't think most of them even noticed the change.

But it wasn't just my work schedule that was upended by those six months of chemotherapy. My whole plan for my future got shook up by Winston and the Clubhouse.

In fact, without cancer, I can safely say that I wouldn't be here in Dallas today, spending my days with the NBA.

My original plan was to work for AT&T for thirty years and then retire. Thirty seemed like a good number, and since I'd started with them when I was just twenty-one, Kenny and I figured it would give me plenty of time for a second career act. After cancer showed me how short and precious life could be, I wanted to free up my time to be more directly involved with my passions.

But my thirty-year anniversary rolled around on the first week I was back after chemo. I'd missed a lot of professional opportunities because of cancer, so I decided to give AT&T one more year.

But God—and AT&T—had other plans.

In the fall of 2012, just as I was getting ready to wind down my career with "the phone company," one of the AT&T executives called. "Your work is done in Raleigh," he said. I agreed with him.

But then he threw a curveball. "We need you at the corporate office," Bill said. It wasn't the first time an executive had suggested that kind of promotion, but I'd always been able to deflect the suggestion because of where the kids were in school, or where I was with my cancer treatment, or whatever else I could come up with. But Shirley was a senior, about to graduate from high school, and Alicia was in her last year of middle school. "Your youngest can start high school in Dallas," he told me. "The timing is perfect."

I didn't want to move. I was getting ready to turn down yet another promotion when he said the words he knew would catch my attention. "We need to change the culture here, Cynt, and you're the one to help do it."

"Boss," I told him, "I've already given you thirty-one years. I have other things I want to do with my life. I don't want to miss my calling just because you need to work on the culture. I need to be pouring into people."

And that's when he got me. "I know what your calling is," he said. "And that's exactly why we need you in Dallas. We need that calling pouring into the people in the halls of AT&T."

Long story short, a vision was spun for me that day of what the company could become, and how I could help with that, and Bill and Randall were so convincing that I agreed not only to put off retirement *again* but also to move to Dallas. Until that point, Kenny and I had planned to stay in North Carolina for good. We were having fun. Our kids loved it. I'd rediscovered my Southern roots. After what we'd been through, North Carolina felt like home.

Texas was something entirely different.

For the next four years, I served as a senior vice president for AT&T, focused on employee engagement, talent management, performance development, diversity, inclusion, and corporate culture all over the country. If my work in North Carolina had been spread thin, getting to know practically everyone in the state, my time at AT&T's corporate office went deep and focused on what happened to the people inside our company walls. My bosses were right; this was a job where I could pour myself into lives and careers. This wasn't a delay of my passion; this *was* my passion. We did something amazing there, and I'm grateful I said yes.

When I *finally* retired in the spring of 2017, after almost thirty-six years at AT&T, I planned to take some time off. Shirley was graduating from college and Alicia was graduating from high school, and I wanted time to catch my breath, help my kids launch into their next seasons, and pray about what would come next. There were a few colleges back in North Carolina making overtures about needing new chancellors or presidents, which sounded appealing.

Instead, the top executive at Dow Chemical called and asked me to help them rework their culture around the principles of diversity, equity, and inclusion. I'd collaborated with their team while I was still at AT&T, and I knew their chairman and executives were committed to the cause but had a monumental task in front of them. I prayed, talked to their staff, and eventually signed on as a consultant. Kenny and I put off moving our empty nest back to North Carolina for a few more months, and I let the universities know I would have to defer a decision for at least a year.

Finally, *finally*, in the spring of 2018, it seemed as if it were the right time to move. Alicia was out of high school and doing her thing. Shirley stayed in North Carolina after college. Anthony was in California. Rickey was living his life in Houston. Kenny and I put an offer on a house in North Carolina and started to get serious about moving back.

But one night, as I came back from another long week of travel and consulting, something in my spirit didn't feel right. As soon as I got home, before I even talked to Kenny, I went straight to my prayer closet.

Yes, I had—and still have—an actual closet in my house that's set aside as my quiet place. When we were younger and the kids were little, I didn't have a dedicated space; the best I could do was lock myself in the bathroom for a few minutes at a time. But eventually, we started living in houses where I had a designated walk-in closet in the hall outside my bedroom, big enough for a chair, my journals and music, cozy blankets that friends have prayed over for me, and a giant tapestry on the wall that was a gift I received during my cancer battle. It's where I go to get away from the noise and spend time listening to the Lord. It's where I have a little church right at home.

As I prayed and listened that night, I felt the Lord telling me not to go to North Carolina. I didn't understand why, but it wasn't time to leave Dallas.

I went downstairs to find Kenny. "Hey, wife," he said before I could start talking, "while you were gone, something came to me. If you're talking about moving back to North Carolina because you think I want to go, that's not it. I don't want to go. I think we should stay in Dallas." He went on to talk about why being in the middle of the country was good for my travel schedule, and that it put us closer to the kids, who were all spread out. From Dallas, we could get to any of our children in three hours. Dallas had been home for a while now, he said, and it was working for us.

I just had to laugh. "Sounds like the Lord's been talking to you, too," I said. We canceled our offer on the house in North Carolina that night.

A week later—really, just a week!—my cellphone rang. I was busy with something else and didn't answer. Then it chimed with a text message. Kenny picked it up, at my request, to see who was trying to get in touch with me, and his eyes got big. "It's Mark Cuban!"

My now-famous response: "Who's that?"

No, I'd never seen *Shark Tank*. I don't have much time for TV.

My kids sure did, though. "Mom, it's Mark Cuban! You have to call him back *right now*." Yes, my husband had already called one of my sons to help persuade me to return the phone call.

I called. Mark and I talked. It was no secret that the Mavericks were in a full-fledged crisis. Their front-office culture was a mess, and the story was national news. My first reaction, when I understood what Mark was asking me, was to wonder why anyone, especially a woman, would want to work there. Why *I* would want to work there. After all, I was trying to retire and make time for the Lord's calling to pour into people!

Mark invited me to come to the office the same afternoon. I told him I would be happy to come, but first I had to go to my mammogram appointment. I'd learned the hard way not to put those things off, after all.

As soon as I met the Mavericks staff, my attitude started to shift. I hadn't even accepted the job, and women were coming up to me in the hallways and telling me their stories. I heard enough on that first day to know that the issues there ran deep. The people I spoke to had been through a lot.

But my conversations with Mark also uncovered his integrity, sincerity, and genuine commitment to making things better from the ground up. He understood that he was in a crisis, and he wanted to fix things. However, he was a guy used to start-up cultures, not organizational redirection. He needed someone with the experience to create operations and systems, as well as a fresh, positive, healthy culture. He also needed someone to pour love and optimism and energy into this staff.

I saw, in an instant, how the Lord had arranged things. How I was, once again, uniquely qualified.

A thirty-seven-year career had taught me how to set up operational systems. A lifetime of challenges, including cancer, had made me bold. And the Lord had called me to use my time and talent to serve others, to invest and pour into the lives of people.

I told Mark I needed to pray about it, and I did. But I think I already knew the answer . . . once again, I had been chosen.

Epilogue

I'll always be grateful that the first person I called when I found out about my cancer was my mother, and that the first thing she said was that this had happened so that I could share the story. I always fully believed that I walked this path, in part, so that I could encourage others. Her words are what prompted me to publish those letters while I was in the middle of the battle. They're why I talk about my cancer in almost every interview and speech I've given in the years since. And they're why you're holding this book in your hands today.

When someone comes to me and says, "I have cancer and I don't know why," I share with them the stories that you've read here, and how I don't believe that there are accidents. Only God knows the complete answer to why He chose colon cancer for me, and not diabetes. Or why He picked me for four second-trimester miscarriages and the loss of my baby, but He spared my husband's life and brought four amazing kids into my family. He put me in a house plagued with domestic violence in the Easter Hill projects, but He also gave me a strong work ethic and a quick mind. Why? I have some guesses, but only He knows for sure. One of my favorite Scriptures is in the book of Jeremiah, where God says, "I know the plans I have for you," but sometimes I have to remind myself that it doesn't also say, "and I'm going to tell you what they all are."

From the day of my first diagnosis, cancer became my touch-point into thousands of lives. And while I know and believe the Lord has a purpose and a plan for everything, that's never been as true as it was when I realized His timing for me in writing this book.

I thought about turning my cancer journal into a book for a long time, especially since it seemed as if people asked me for one on a weekly basis. But as you've seen, life kept me busy. There were new jobs, big moves, and plenty of other ways I was living my calling. I had to be content to print copies of the original journal entries and give them to anyone who wanted to know about my cancer battle.

But there was always this whisper in the back of my head. *There's so much more to this story. There's so much more that you need to say.*

Finally, after almost a decade of obstacles and false starts, things came together and I started to write in earnest.

I was just a couple of chapters in when a close member of my staff, David, approached me one night at the end of a Mavericks home game and asked if I had a few minutes to talk.

Honestly? I didn't. It had been a long day, one of many in a long year, and I was tired. All I wanted was to get to my car and get home. But I liked David. He was our chief technology officer, and we spent a lot of time together. Of everyone who works at the Mavs, in fact, I'd probably spent more hours with him than anyone else.

I already knew, because I ask everyone I work with about their life stories, that David was smitten with his girlfriend, Michelle. That night he told me Michelle had just found out she had stage 4 colon cancer. His eyes were big, and I remembered that initial, dazed feeling, when everything you think you know about your future is turned upside down. The love of his life needed chemo and the whole range of treatments, but Michelle didn't have health insurance. David was thinking about speeding up his plans to marry her so that he could help her financially, as well as emotionally, walk through this battle. What did I think?

Well, of course I thought it was wonderful. He was dedicated and obviously in love. David was a hero, and I offered to help them in any way I could.

Their February wedding, coming in the middle of the COVID-19 pandemic, was small, but their love was huge. Over the next few months, I saw David become a true partner in his wife's cancer journey, and they both became tied more closely to my life. There were just so many parallels with my experiences.

Michelle started chemo on an every-other-week schedule, with the pump for an extra two days, just as I had. David took her to every appointment and every round of chemo. He would often call me with questions about cancer, or just dial the phone and then hand it to Michelle so I could talk to her about what she was going through. Since I was in the middle of writing this book, all of my experiences were right in front of me. There were plenty of times when I was reviewing chapters and thought about how I needed to tell David to pick up some fluffy socks, or ask about how Michelle was doing with the noise her pump made.

Then, on the Wednesday before Easter, my phone rang, and it wasn't David. It was someone else from our office, calling to tell me that David had passed away, tragically and completely unexpectedly, from a heart attack. He was only fifty-seven years old.

Michelle, of course, was beyond devastated. Here she was, newly wed and fighting for her own life, and she had lost her husband. For months, all of their attention had been on her survival, not his. She'd just moved to Dallas and didn't know anyone here, unless her medical team counted.

There wasn't time to ask why. There was only time to think

"what next." I met Michelle that afternoon and took her home with me. The next morning, I took her to her chemo appointment. I arranged for her family to fly in to be with her, and I helped them make funeral arrangements. My boss said, "Give them whatever they need." The Lord used him, too.

Each step of those surreal, wild, heavy weeks paralleled these pages as I relived the grief of losing my child, the comfort of my Clubhouse community, and everything in between. I felt her shock and then the paralyzing heaviness of her grief as I wrote about my own. Watching her reminded me of things I wanted to share with you all about the relentlessness of a cancer battle and the importance of the village. I revisited all of it as I held the hand of this sweet, grieving woman.

Talk about being uniquely equipped and chosen for a situation!

Yes, I believe there is a reason for everything, and that includes my battle with colon cancer as well as the timing of this book that's now, finally, in your hands. All I can do is shake my head, because I was meant to write it exactly when I did and to be in this specific place and with these people, as Scripture says, for such a time as this.

If you have been diagnosed with cancer,
I pray for your recovery.

If you are the spouse of someone who is fighting
this battle of a lifetime, I pray for your strength.

If your mother or father has been told they have
cancer, I pray for optimism, togetherness, and a
degree of family normalcy.

If one of your employees, co-workers, business
associates, or customers needs support for this
journey, I pray that you do SOMETHING, as every
gesture warms the heart like a blanket.

If one of your patients has cancer and you're not
the oncologist, please embrace the uniqueness of
this treatment and learn more about chemotherapy.

If a close friend tells you they have cancer,
I pray that you will invade their space.

If you read about someone's diagnosis, I pray that
you will send them a note of encouragement.

If you notice shedding hair, a flying fork,
or hot drinks and fluffy socks in the summer,
just start praying. You could possibly have
discovered a new member of the cancer clubhouse.
Feel free to join their team! You do indeed have a
most valuable role to play.

Rick's Navy Bean Soup

So many people over the years have asked about my friend Rick Smith's navy bean soup, which he generously made for me throughout my chemo and which was often the only thing I could keep down. I asked him to share the recipe, and he graciously agreed. Rick says:

"This recipe was adapted from my mother, who got it from her mother, who made it in the 1930s and 1940s. It was always a comfort food for me growing up."

Ingredients

1 pound dried navy beans
8-plus cups water
2 pounds ham hocks
  (or any leftover ham)
1 cup chopped white onion
2 cups thin-sliced carrots
1 cup chopped celery
1 bay leaf

½ teaspoon black pepper
½ teaspoon oregano
1 teaspoon salt (depending on
  salt content of ham)
1 teaspoon basil
¼ cup fresh parsley
8 cups chicken or vegetable
  broth (low sodium)

Rinse and sort the beans. Place in a big pot and cover with water to at least two inches or so above the beans. Bring to a boil and boil for three minutes. Cover and simmer for an additional hour until the beans are softened.

Drain and rinse the beans, and discard the water. Add the beans back to the pot along with all the broth, onion, parsley, ham, and seasonings. Bring to a boil, cover, and simmer for an hour. The beans should be tender.

Add the carrots and celery and mix. Cover and simmer on low heat for thirty minutes, then remove the ham and the bay leaf. Chop up the ham once it is cool enough to do so. Remove a few cups of the beans and mash/chop them to paste consistency, and return the ham and mashed beans back to the pot and stir. Depending on the consistency you like, increase or decrease the amount of beans used to thicken. Heat and serve.

Acknowledgments

WE DID IT! We beat cancer and wrote a book about it!

After ten years of sending my "Winston and the Clubhouse" journal to people who were touched by cancer, my chemo story (and more) is finally available to encourage the masses.

This is my first book. I started working on it during airplane rides in 2018, and a year later, I presented what I thought was a masterpiece. Thank you, Jan Miller, for insisting that I hand it over and for graciously turning it into what God meant it to be, a story about His amazing grace and goodness. Mary Reynics, thank you for making me take you and your team through my journey. You made me realize that God didn't just meet me at the oncologist's office. He had shown up, faithful and forceful, so many times and in so many years prior to equip me to fight cancer. I had indeed been chosen—time and time again.

Beth Jusino, you are beyond magnificent. I thought I gave you something that required very little work. You came back week in and week out with words on paper that made me cry, smile, and run around my house. You have been blessed with extraordinary writing skills. Sister, I will always cherish our virtual Friday night chats.

Carolyn "Ma" Gardner, I thank the Lord daily that He gave me you for my mother. Not only are you a wonderful role model of resiliency, grace, and grit, but you have always encouraged me to tell the gritty stories. You told me that my getting cancer was for His glory, and one day I would boldly tell the story. Your prophecy is now in your hands. Enjoy what is not just His story but YOUR story, too.

Kenny, Rickey, Anthony (aka Ken), Shirley, and Alicia, I am honored to have had you by my side as prayer warriors and caretakers. You served in whatever role I needed y'all to play. The Lord put our family together, and it was clear to me during this fight that our family was a force to be reckoned with. We just seem to know how to rally the troops and handle difficult things. Thank you for showing up for me during one of the toughest times of my life. My chemo brain, pain, fatigue, or sleeping on the floor in a fetal position never kept you away. You always showed up. Even when the chemo pump and ports were gone and no one was watching, y'all were still getting me to my regular oncology appointments on time, accommodating the still-lingering after-effects, and treating me like the Queen of the Castle. Thank you for accepting weakened taste buds, bald spots to cover up, neuropathy, and a compromised immune system. Knowing that you unconditionally love the new me means everything!

Smith kids (aka my siblings), you gave real meaning to "ride or die." From our childhood bond to the unexpected visits to North Carolina to the round-the-clock fasting and praying, thank you for never leaving the middle one stuck in the middle. Ben and Gynelle, I will always remember how you took my case to the altar. Cameron, your braving the weather and showing up in Raleigh is etched in my mind. Our white Christmas was special because of you. Marshall crew, thank you for your prayers and support.

Thank you, AT&T family. Thousands of T sisters and brothers offered me more love than I could handle. You brought my theme song to life and showed me every day that there really wasn't a mountain high enough to keep y'all from getting to me. Patrick Zimmerman, Micki Burton, and others, your stroke of genius to bring us 919Dine relieved me of the stress of caring for my family. You have no idea what that gesture meant to me. I can't even begin to describe your love for me, but hopefully you will smile as you uncover the nuggets within these pages. Sylvia Russell, Venessa Harrison, Rob Smith, Clifton Metcalf, and Connie Bragg, I will always be grateful for how you made it okay for me to be sick. To all my bosses, and you know who you are, thanks for making my healthcare needs and my family a priority. Bill Blase, I will never forget sitting in the parking lot at the surgeon's office listening to your message that I BETTER call you because you had to hear my voice. You and Randall role-modeled caring leadership in a very special way. Fassil Fenikile and Robin MacGillivray, your daily talks with God made a difference. And of course, Robin, the big church lady hat gave me shade in more ways than one.

My friends at the North Carolina Chamber, Lew Ebert, John Simpson, Billie Redmond, Kelly King, and Patty B, you just jumped in and handled it. You didn't care that you had only forty-eight hours of notice to cover for me. Thank you for taking a big responsibility off my plate so smoothly and quickly. Erskine, thank you for excusing my absence. President Obama, thank you for your prayers and for understanding my weakened state.

Julia Howard and the North Carolina legislature, getting Maya Angelou and Robin Kaplan Thaler to sign my favorite books really did lift my spirits. Mission accomplished.

Governor Bev Perdue, you were one of the first people to pray for me. Thank you for your friendship and encouragement.

My Research Triangle neighbors, my regulator friends, and the North Carolina community, I love you so much. You embraced my family and showed hospitality in a way that will always make me smile. Something was always on our doorstep.

Reverend Dr. William Barber, you showed up with a prayer that called down heaven. Thank you for letting the Spirit lead you and for doing what the Lord commanded you to do that night. You left me much better than you found me. My California pastors, Phil Howard and Big Dave, thank you for the prayers that I truly felt in my bones.

To the sisterhood across North Carolina, California, Texas, New York, Georgia, New Jersey, Washington, D.C., and the world, thank you for the chemo pearls, fluffy socks, prayer blankets, tapestries, and family activity ideas (y'all knew that the being-at-home thing was foreign to me). Carol Wilner and Jo Anne Rashbaum, your kindness made a difference. I am still wearing the fluffy socks.

Aime Hadnot, thank you for surprising me and creatively binding the first "Winston and the Clubhouse" journal. You caused me to pay attention to how often people called, and made me realize the importance of sharing my cancer story.

North Carolina media, thank you for the compassionate and patient way you told my story. Rick Smith (WRAL), your story is my story, and you used our stories to change lives. *The News & Observer* (Raleigh), you and many others told my story with grace and purpose. Thank you. It's as if you knew about my mother's prophecy.

Thank you to the other Rick Smith for his special homemade navy bean soup. I appreciate you for allowing us to share it with the world.

To my posse, my girls, my "let's roll out" buddies: Yvonne, Hokey, Lisa, Bev. Thank you, divas, for rolling in at the beginning and for rolling out to the Clubhouse, and for doing whatever was necessary (and sometimes unnecessary). Y'all took care of me and my family in ways I will never forget. I probably actually remember more of it now. Sarah, we share more than a birthday. We share chemo memories that will last a lifetime. Thank you for showing up.

Jonathan Bow and Crosspointe Church, you activated and responded and showed my children why being part of a church family is essential. Pastor, thank you for dropping everything to come to our house to comfort my spirit. You made it okay for me to be vulnerable and scared. You prayed when I was at a loss for words.

To all of you who joined me on this journey and your name is not mentioned here, you will find yourself in the journal postings that I urge you to read or in the surrounding stories.

To the incredible medical team at the Cancer Centers of North Carolina, I don't have enough words to describe what you mean to me. Dr. Charlie Eisenbeis, the Lord gave you something special to share with others. You are more than a brilliant oncologist. Your leadership and compassion permeated the walls of the CCNC. Thank you for believing in the miracle that had yet to unfold. Thank you for allowing me to turn the infusion suite into a partying clubhouse. Thank you for taking Benadryl out of my regimen so that I could enjoy day one of chemo as long as I possibly could. Thank you for letting me think I was in charge even when I could barely function. And thank you and Robin for checking on my family and showing up once we found out we were neighbors, especially when the garage caught on fire. Thank you to the amazing and dedicated nurses and medical staff. I will forever cherish our time together. You went above and beyond to care for me and many others while also decorating and dressing up for theme parties. I can't begin to express my gratitude for how you saved my life.

Finally, to all of you who are reading these acknowledgments, thank you. This book is in your hands for a reason. Someone's journey through adversity is beginning. Another person's journey continues. Perhaps you're helping someone make it to the finish line. Or maybe, just maybe, your journey has begun. You've been chosen!

About the Author

CYNTHIA "CYNT" MARSHALL is the CEO of the Dallas Mavericks, president and CEO of Marshalling Resources consulting, and the former senior vice president of human resources and chief diversity officer for AT&T. She is the first Black woman to hold the CEO role for any NBA team. She is also an outspoken cancer survivor, regular speaker at cancer-related events, and vocal supporter of cancer patients and their families across the country. The fourth of six children, Marshall grew up in Richmond, California, and lives in the Dallas area. She and her husband, Kenneth, have four adult children.

Twitter: @cyntmarshall

About the Type

This book was set in Garamond, a typeface originally designed by the Parisian type cutter Claude Garamond (c. 1500–61). This version of Garamond was modeled on a 1592 specimen sheet from the Egenolff-Berner foundry, which was produced from types assumed to have been brought to Frankfurt by the punch cutter Jacques Sabon (c. 1520–80).

Claude Garamond's distinguished romans and italics first appeared in *Opera Ciceronis* in 1543–44. The Garamond types are clear, open, and elegant.